THE HUNT FOR HOME

A Korean-American Family Memoir

Kyong Suk Han Richardson

COPYRIGHT

The Hunt for Home
Kyong Suk Han Richardson, 2019

Scripture quotations are taken from the *Holy Bible, New International Version. NIV* copyright © 1973, 1978, 1984 by the International Bible Society.

ISBN: 978-0-578-58734-9

Cover Design: Katie Montalto, KM Creative

Printed in the U.S.A

1st Edition

To my boys,
all I've ever wanted was to do right by you;
but, you doing right by me is what has been true.

CONTENTS

FOREWORD
By Michael Caviness

My brother, Robert, and I cannot be more excited about this family memoir. Over the years, we've heard so many profound stories from my mom's childhood, and I have had the privilege of watching her grow into the family matriarch she has become today. I don't use the term matriarch to imply my mom is some type of domineering woman. She is the opposite. She is kindhearted, self-less, but yes, also a bit strong-willed.

It's been said that one of the greatest travesties in humanity is when a family's stories die with someone who never shared them. History is not only interesting; it is instrumental. My mom's name is Kyong Suk Han Richardson, or Suki for short. We are so grateful for mom's courage in sharing her stories, for they are our family's history.

The only regret we all carry about this memoir is that it wasn't written sooner. If it had been, my Harmony (Mom's mom), Jennifer Senter, Joyce Kinney, and many other loved ones who have passed would surely have contributed and added so much flavor to the stories held within these pages.

The purposes of this memoir are important to share. First, Mom would say she wants to give all glory to God. Second, she hopes to encourage her family. Third, without quite realizing she's doing so, she is leaving a legacy of faith and grit within these pages. The inspiration her stories provoke in anyone who is willing to sit and listen (or read), even for a few moments, is powerful. We knew we wanted to— no, we realized we needed to—ensure her stories would be accurately passed down from generation to generation. Robert and I know the power of our family's past, paired with mom's humility in telling it, will benefit not only our family but countless others who may find the opportunity to read this memoir.

FAMILY TREE

This memoir is written by Kyong Suk Han Richardson with contributions from her sons, Michael and Robert Caviness, her daughter-in-law, Dawn Caviness, and her granddaughter, Adia Caviness.

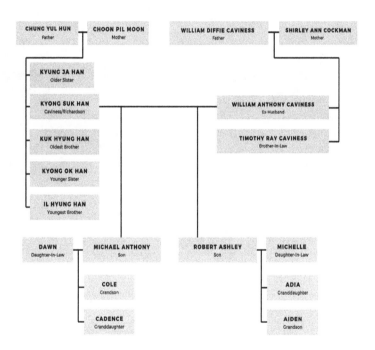

PART I

LOST HOME

"Jesus knew their thoughts and said to them, 'Every kingdom divided against itself will be ruined, and every city or household divided against itself will not stand." —Matthew 12:25

PROLOGUE

Hungnam-guyok, North Korea
1948

The tiny fifteen-year-old girl boldly presented her ticket and boarded the train to Munchon, North Korea, situated sixty-five miles to the south. She had been counting down the days to her trip back to the countryside, longing to spend time with her mother and father. It had been a year since she had last seen her parents and siblings. It was a hard twelve months.

Three years prior—in August 1945—the Soviet Union had invaded Korea, which had been under Japan's control since 1910. Fearing the Soviets' intentions of seizing the entire peninsula for their own gain, the United States quickly moved its troops into the southern regions of Korea. In an effort to avoid a long-term conflict within its borders, the United States and the U.S.S.R. agreed to temporarily divide Korea along the 38th parallel, bisecting the country. This line became permanent after 1946 when leaders in the northern half organized a communist government. Shortly after, a nationalist exile set up a rival government in the south. Each new government hoped to reunify the country under its own rule. Fighting erupted amid the growing tension between the two leaders. Every Korean felt the tension.

The girl took an empty window seat on the train and settled in for the ninety-minute ride. Deep into the journey, the train unexpectedly stopped when the engineer noticed debris blocking the track ahead and hit the brakes. The conductor directed every passenger, including the young teenager, off the train. They discovered an explosion had damaged the rails. With no other options, the mass of passengers and crew began to walk along the track in the nighttime darkness, seeking out the next closest station.

When the sun hid below the horizon, the temperature dropped. The passengers wrapped their arms around themselves. Then without warning, bombs began to fall around them. They sprinted to a nearby ditch and lay down in the cold grass. The girl heard screams as she recoiled from the continued explosions. In a wave of clarity, she realized the screams were her own. She reached up and covered her head with her hands and sank further into the trench.

As quickly as the bombing started, it ceased. The passengers tentatively stood up, brushed the dirt from their clothes, and wiped the fear from their eyes. Everyone had survived. Without any other options, they continued to walk through the night.

The girl reached her parent's village the next day. Her feet were blistered and her hips ached, but she had enough energy to hug her parents tightly.

After a short visit, she returned to the train station. There seemed to be a break in the bombing, and most people hoped the conflict was over. The trains were running on schedule again. The teenager waved goodbye and safely returned to Hungnam-guyok.

      She never saw her parents again.

1 | WAR

I was an adult before I learned the story of how my mother escaped North Korea. My mother shared her childhood experiences and described the terror she felt as both a child and adolescent after coming to live with me in the United States from 1985 to 1995. Her life—our lives—had been difficult in Korea, and it wasn't until she moved here, to this country, that she was able to talk about her childhood.

To look at my little, bitty mother, one would never have imagined she carried a strong-willed and brave personality. She stood a mere four feet, ten inches tall. Yet, she was every bit a feisty, courageous, and independent individual. Her name was Choon Pil Moon.

Choon Pil was born in 1933 in northern Korea when Japan had already occupied the country for twenty-three years. Japan worked hard to wipe out Korean culture, language, and history. My mother's first language was Japanese, and just as with all Korean children at the time, she was forced to attend Japanese schools. Whenever the Japanese military rolled into town, most parents hid their daughters in makeshift basements in their houses. The reason for this was because the soldiers often took girls for "labor" purposes. Koreans had lived in fear for decades. This was the world of my mother's childhood.

After thirty-six comprehensive years, Japanese occupation of Korea ended in 1945 when U.S. and Soviet forces captured the peninsula. It was then, after Japan lost Word War II, my mother began to learn her native language. She was thirteen years old.

Living in the town of Munchon—in the countryside—she didn't have much opportunity to receive an education. Most girls were denied school-based learning because of the cost and the fact that Korean culture gave boys preferential treatment. Yet, she wanted to pursue her education. She knew it was the window of opportunity. Therefore, when my mother was fourteen years old, she left the countryside and moved to the city of Hungnam on the eastern coast of northern Korea. Her parents remained in Munchon. She lived at a factory school close to her older sister's family. She worked during the day and attended classes at night.

Soon after this move, her world changed again. Not long after Koreans breathed a sigh of relief after having rid themselves of their Japanese oppressors, more conflict brewed within the country. By the end of 1948, the conflict had caused Korea to split into what we now know as North and South Korea.

The Korean War officially began in June 1950, eighteen months after my mom's harrowing train ride to see her parents. Six months later, the Chinese entered North Korea, fanning out from the northern and western parts of the country and pushing civilians and U.S. Forces toward the port city of Hungnam. The Chinese troops accused Koreans of assisting UN (United Nations) and American forces, giving themselves permission to destroy whole towns and cities as they made their way down and across the peninsula.

During one of the coldest winters in Korean history, on December 22, my mother fled her home in the heart of Hungnam and escaped to the nearby harbor. She left behind most everything she owned, with the exception of the clothes on her back and whatever possessions would fit in her pockets or the small bag she draped over her shoulder. Seventeen-year-old Choon Pil wasn't alone. She, her sister, her brother-in-law, and her two nephews joined 98,000 other Koreans pressing into Hungnam Harbor. Their collective hope was to board waiting American ships, escape into the sea, and avoid annihilation. The United States promised the Koreans they would bring them back to North Korea in two weeks—once the fighting ended.

The beach at the harbor became crowded with lines of families seeking safety. Ten thousand Korean refugees streamed onto each available ship. It took twenty-four hours to board everyone. Once on board, there was no space to move. Some hung from the sides of the ships, desperately trying to avoid falling into the water below. There was no place to lie down, let alone sleep. Later, American seamen on the U.S.S. Missouri described what they saw from their warship moored in the harbor.

"The boats that passed us were crowded with humanity."[1]

The ship carrying my mother, the U.S.S. Meredith Victory, would later be referred to as the

---

[1] *Chosin*, directed by Brian Iglesias (2010; USA: Veterans Expeditionary Media and Post Factory Films, 2010), DVD.

"Ship of Miracles." It was the last ship to leave Hungnam Harbor and held the largest number of people—nearly 14,000 souls. As a final and desperate measure, demolition teams destroyed the harbor within hours of the mass evacuation. They were intent on keeping the Chinese from using the port for themselves.

> "Never in recorded history have combatants rescued so many civilians from enemy territory in the midst of battle. It is estimated that over one million descendants of these stoic and courageous Koreans, whom we rescued, are living productive lives in Korea today."
> —Rear Admiral Lunney

The U.S.S. Meredith Victory landed in Busan, South Korea on December 24, 1950. Miraculously, everyone survived. However, the ship was turned away because the port was already full with refugees from other boats that had landed there first. They sailed to an island further south where Choon Pil Moon, her family, and the 14,000 others stepped on South Korean soil and entered a refugee camp. They held tight to the promise of returning to their homes soon. Sadly, they never did get that chance, and my mother never saw her parents again.

My mother and her sister's family eventually moved to a tent city set up for refugees in Busan. Her brother-in-law was sick, so my mother worked to help support her sister's family, taking odd jobs whenever she could find them. She also cared for her nephews while her sister worked. They were simply surviving, along with the almost one hundred thousand others who had fled North Korea and found themselves living in what had become the world's newest, and poorest, country.

This is only half of the story—my mother's side. My father had a story, too. Chung Yul Han was a tall and handsome man. He was born into a prominent family in northern Korea, much like what we would refer to today as a dynasty. They were wealthy and influential. As with all Korean family names, those with the Han surname are divided into different bloodlines, known as bon-gwan. From my understanding, the Han name has been in Korea for over one thousand years.

Chung Yul was married and had fathered two children (a boy and a girl) but separated from his wife prior to 1950—a fact my mother didn't learn until after they were married. He had been living in northern Korea in Humhong. His job was to buy goods and travel to the south to exchange them for a profit. As was the case for all those in northern Korea, the growing conflict changed his life too. To avoid being forced to serve as a communist soldier, my daddy snuck out of the country. He fled North Korea to join his sister-in-law, their two children, and the other refugees in Busan. It was 1952.

This next part of the family story was passed down to me from my sister, so I share the details as they were told to me.

After a couple of months, my daddy's brother announced his desire to return to their homeland to find the rest of the Han family. Everyone decided his wife and sons should stay with my dad. They were never reunited. No one knows what happened to my uncle.

My dad's sister-in-law introduced him to Choon Pil Moon, my mother, in the tent city. They were married soon after meeting. My sister, Kyung Ja Han, was born in 1953 there in Busan. My mother was twenty years old at the time. I was born in 1955. My given name is Kyong Suk Han, hence my nickname, Suki.

Just prior to my second birthday, my parents sought out a more permanent place to settle down and call home. A tent city is no place for any family to live—certainly not for more than two years. My mom's sister's family moved to Seoul in the northwestern corner of South Korea, and my parents followed. We were all looking for better opportunities, searching for better lives. Daddy became a truck driver, and we settled into our new city. So began our family life.

2 | THE CITY

In Seoul, our family grew. My parents had three additional children, totaling five. First came the third girl of the family, Kyong Ok Han. Then, my mother bore her two boys. The oldest son is Kuk Hyung Han and the baby of the family is Il Hyung Han.

Growing up, I learned a few things from my daddy. I learned a life lived well is filled with fun. I like to think I became a generous person by watching him give so freely when I was young. When we ran into a needy family, he always helped them. If a neighbor was sick, he took them rice or some other food. He taught me that when we have, we should give.

A special memory I cherish is of the day my dad came home from work when I was four years old to find I had been suffering with a bellyache all day. He cradled me in his arms and took me to get cider. I loved him for seeing me and caring for me in that way—so much so that my stomach pain faded away. I'll never forget the words he uttered while the last sip of cider was still on my tongue.

"You're my girl."

Every child should hear such words. I remember them as if they were spoken yesterday, despite being a little bitty thing when he said them to me.

I treasure the times he lined up the three girls and asked us to sing together. He enjoyed listening to our voices as we harmonized and giggled. We enjoyed seeing him smile. I wish those moments I loved most about him remained unfailing throughout my childhood, but they didn't.

I don't think my dad ever stopped loving his former wife. He missed her. It seemed he couldn't let go of his memories and feelings of his first family. Rather than moving forward and embracing his new family, he became what Americans call a womanizer. He also started drinking. My father was big-hearted and open-handed, but eventually, he became an alcoholic and his support of the family grew inconsistent.

My daddy wanted his children to be strong and do the right things even while he wasn't. He would work one or two days and then take off for several days, using the money he had earned for more alcohol. It became a devastating cycle that offered us no stability or security in our home. It was difficult to understand why he stopped looking after us, but I have a guess.

Our life as refugees in Busan, and then as transplants in Seoul, was difficult. As the son of a wealthy and powerful family, my daddy took his circumstances particularly hard. He became bitter and ornery. He must have thought he was failing his family of origin, mishandling a generational legacy, or dishonoring his family name. He couldn't accept the tough hand he was dealt. As I think about that, I can see—in a way—why he did what he did. As a child, that didn't stop me from thinking it wasn't fair. What about this family, our family?

While my daddy self-destructed, the children became my mother's priority. She worked any job she could find to keep food on our table. Sometimes, she would clean and fold laundry for other families. Other times, she worked in the vegetable fields. Her words tried to convince us the next year would be better, but the long days and her worn face said otherwise. It seemed she had leaned on that mantra for her whole life: next year will be better. My mother was a tough woman. Without her, we never would have made it. She did well keeping us safe and close, at least for a while.

Without getting too far ahead in this memoir, I spent years watching my mother make sacrifices and put her children first. I guess that is how I learned to love my two boys.

"There's no way I'm going to lose you," she promised us.

I watched her set aside her dreams and forgo her own time and heart to ensure we had everything we needed. In no simple terms, those things included hope, food, and a work ethic that paralleled no one else I've ever known. My mother was brave and determined, and I like to think I inherited those things from her. I hope I have mothered my boys as well as she mothered us.

In Seoul, we ultimately landed at my aunt and her family's house in a city neighborhood. Times were tough, and my aunt convinced my mom that I should go stay with a Buddhist lady she knew. This lady had no children of her own, and my parents decided it would be best if she raised me. They tried to convince me it would be a better life. I can only guess the real motivation was they would have one less mouth to feed. They dropped me off, but I wouldn't stay. I was only six years old, but I knew how to find my way back to my family's home. I kept running away and returning home, so eventually they all gave up. I moved back in with Mom and Daddy. Even though I was allowed to stay home, I felt like it was too easy for them to just give me away in the first place. That left a scar.

A short time later, my aunt asked our family to leave her house because of my daddy's behavior. He was still pursuing his destructive ways, slipping in and out of the house at all hours, running around with other people, and drinking. My aunt wanted no part of it.

My mother was terrified of trying to care for three daughters on her own (my brothers had not yet been born), so she sent me off with my dad and kept my older sister, who had already entered school, and my baby sister with her. My aunt permitted the three of them to return, and my daddy and I went back to Busan. We stayed with my daddy's sister-in-law, and I did without my mom. Feeling rejected and alone, I grieved as I sat with a growing sense of unworthiness.

A few months later, my daddy must have convinced my aunt and mother that he could do better because we found ourselves back home. My heart and spirit were still broken. I had learned that my family's love was conditional and depended on our financial resources. I lived in fear that at any moment, I might be abandoned over my siblings' safety and security or my dad's choices. The feelings of being small and unloved became etched into my heart.

I started school soon after our return to the house. At that time, there was no such thing as kindergarten in South Korea, so I entered the first grade. We lived next to a Christian family with a daughter about my age. This was interesting because my aunt was a fortune-teller. Yes, there was a church-going family living next door to a fortune-teller! I chuckle now as I think about what that family must have thought about all the random people coming in and out of our house.

One day during the Christmas season, our neighbors asked us to go to church with them. We had never been a religious family. Though, from my earliest memories, my mother had always encouraged us to go to church. She had learned about Christianity from missionaries in the refugee camp of her childhood. My mother knew it would be good for us to go to church, to learn about God, and sing the songs she had once sung—songs such as "The Solid Rock." Thinking about the lyrics now, I imagine they were a powerful source of comfort for her and the other refugees in Busan.

"THE SOLID ROCK"
A hymn of grace by Edward Mote (1863)

My hope is built on nothing less
Than Jesus' blood and righteousness;
I dare not trust the sweetest frame,
But wholly lean on Jesus' name.

When darkness veils His lovely face,
I rest on His unchanging grace;
In every high and stormy gale,
My anchor holds within the veil.

His oath, His covenant, His blood

Support me in the whelming flood;
When all around my soul gives way,
He then is all my hope and stay.

When He shall come with trumpet sound,
Oh, may I then in Him be found;
Dressed in His righteousness alone,
Faultless to stand before the throne.

Refrain:
On Christ, the solid Rock, I stand;
All other ground is sinking sand,
All other ground is sinking sand.

At the time, I didn't know why Christians did what they did at Christmas. I did not understand the significance of bringing a tree into the home and decorating it. I thought the tree, much like the tradition of decorating boiled eggs at Easter, was just for fun. The church we attended was a Presbyterian church a missionary had built. I don't know where Christian Koreans would be today without so many missionaries flooding our shores so many years ago.

I ended up attending the church for two years. My memory had always been of walking down and across several busy city streets to get there. As a child, I lamented the long journey. When I returned to South Korea in 2018, I walked by the church again. It was much closer to our old neighborhood than my memories had always led me to believe. Sometimes, our childhood perspectives are like that, aren't they?

The church is now well over one hundred years old. It was erected of solid rock, and is larger than it used to be when I lived in Seoul. They've built additional wings and updated the front door. I realized while looking at it through adult eyes I had never forgotten the church itself. The bell at the top of the building played piano music two times each day. The first was at 5:00 a.m. to wake people up and then again at 10:00 p.m. to alert everyone it was time to go to bed. As I gazed at that church, I remembered the music, and it made me smile. The hymns were lovely, and everyone living in that part of town could hear them.

After several weeks of attending church with our neighbors, I caught myself enjoying the children's service. It was held deep in the basement. I couldn't read, but I followed along as they turned the pages of the hymnals while we sang. I still recall the words to some of the songs. God used these neighbors to plant His first seed in my soul.

3 | THE COUNTRY

In 1963, the city of Seoul embraced a new mission. City officials began to tear down much of the area where my family lived. Construction crews leveled buildings at lightening speeds as the South Korean government aimed to improve the city's infrastructure (in an effort to overcome the economic challenges the country faced). Even the United States noticed Seoul's changing landscape. "Chosun Hotel, a Seoul Landmark, Will Be Razed For a New Skyscraper," ran a *New York Times* headline in 1966. Our house did not escape Seoul's forward progress. The building we called home was scheduled for demolition, and we were forced to move again.

My family members and I packed up our meager belongings, and we headed for the country. For the second time in our lives, we lived in a tent surrounded by hundreds of other families squeezed into their own makeshift shelters. These tents were actually tarps on wooden stakes. There was no electricity and no clean water.

As a third-grader, I thought our move was fun. I didn't recognize how desperate a situation we faced, and I certainly didn't understand why my mom couldn't stop crying. I couldn't comprehend the painful fact that my parents had lost their home—again. In my youthful naivety, I thought, *How exciting! We're camping!* A river flowed nearby the "campgrounds" and I spent countless hours playing in the water, climbing on the rocks, and hiking through the hills. It was within this season of my life I discovered I was a country girl at heart, and for perhaps the first time in my life, my heart felt free.

In the summertime, particularly in the monsoon season of June, the tent city flooded. The drainage areas were often clogged with trash, debris, and waste. The smell of rotten food permeated the whole area. I remember one awful night; we all woke up to water rushing into our tent. Within seconds, it was knee-deep. My dad and others ran to the drainage ditch to clear it so the river would stop flowing into our shelters. They used their bare hands to clean it all out. They must have been gagging.

My sister and I were tasked with taking the laundry to the river and washing it. We would stay there all day, swimming and climbing on the rocks. Then, we would scamper back to the tent for dinner, hungry and exhausted from all our activity. We even built ourselves a little house out of the river rocks. We were so happy in those moments as we dreamed of a day when we might have a real house to call our own.

Eventually, a neighbor installed a pump well near our shelters. It became our small cluster of tents' water supply, and the kids thought it was so much fun to own the chore of pumping clean water for our families. We were grateful for those neighbors.

Gratitude became one of my lifelong virtues during this time in my life. To this day, I experience physical pain when I see anything being wasted or thrown away—food, clothes, or furniture. You name it. I probably tend to hoard it. I am the proverbial pack rat. *Someone may need this some day.*

Unfortunately, this move to the country meant I had to stop attending the church I had grown to love. Thankfully, a Korean preacher brought our community a tent church. The church held Vacation Bible School (VBS) for the kids the summer between my third and fourth grade years. It was a branch of a much larger church from the city. During VBS, I learned how to worship. We didn't have any toys, but the VBS volunteers brought paper, scissors, and crayons to do arts and crafts. They gifted us with small booklets containing the gospels, printed from somewhere far away. They didn't have the money to give each child a whole Bible.

Living in the countryside also meant I had to walk five miles to the bus stop and rode two busses just to get to school. My sister and I made this two-hour trek (each direction) together for two years, but when she graduated the sixth grade, I was no longer allowed to go. It wasn't safe for me to travel alone. I was pulled out of the city school after fourth grade and enrolled in the nearby countryside school. I remained there for fifth and sixth grade.

Sixth grade graduation signified the end of elementary school in 1960's Korea—the end of the education journey for many girls. Schooling was a privilege at this time in Korean history, not a right. All schools were tuition-based. Elementary schools required a nominal fee, but my parents could not afford to pay my middle school tuition. They were already paying for my older sister to attend. I was thirteen years old when I left school, but I longed to continue my education. Like my mother before me, I dreamed of a better life with more opportunities, but it just didn't seem to be an option for me.

Contempt and anger toward my parents grew, and I blamed them for my inability to pursue my education. I was already feeling forgotten as I lived through the injustice of being a second-born girl in Korean culture and from the memory of being castoff when my dad was kicked out of the house years earlier. I made the decision to leave home and stay with my aunt, my mother's sister, who had moved further into the country when our house was demolished. Not long after I left, my parents moved back to Seoul.

It was not easy living with my aunt. She had rheumatic fever as a child—a common illness in Korea in the middle of the century—and she struggled with subsequent heart problems. There wasn't adequate medical care or enough medication available, so she was often sick. My aunt's family raised goats in the countryside as a means to make a living. I helped my cousin care for the family goats as reciprocation for my room and board.

I lived with my aunt's family for several months. It was an eye-opening season. For the first time, I felt needed. It was a sharp contrast to what I experienced at home, where I was not important–an afterthought. At home, no one bragged about me. No one praised me. I was a lonesome girl. At the farm, I was helpful and felt appreciated for the work I did. I knew I was making a difference for my aunt.

While living with my aunt, nature shocked Korea with a cold winter, and my mom called for me to return home. I had no choice. I packed my bag and made my way back to their home, which was now a place located just outside Seoul's city limits but still considered to be part of the countryside back then. I didn't allow myself to feel much about returning. Without a safe outlet, I was learning how to suppress uncomfortable feelings. It was my responsibility as a young teenager to help provide for my family.

Since Korean culture, and by extension my parents, expected me to work to support the family, I found a job in a factory that made matches. My older sister, Kyung Ja, was still in middle school. This was also acceptable in the eyes of culture. First-born children were gifted with more opportunities in education, jobs, families, and society as a whole. I found the factory job through friends and neighbors who worked there. When my sister heard I had started working in the factory, she quit school and joined me. She was a good big sister.

The factory was lit only by what came through the windows during the day. After the sun went down, the overhead lights flickered on. The smell of the factory, a chemical odor that stayed with me after I left each day, is still vivid in my memory. I was responsible for folding the thick paper into a fan, accordion-style, and cutting the folded paper by hand into the long pieces that would eventually become matches sold to restaurants.

However, there were many times I labored alongside my co-workers in the other steps of the manufacturing process. There were days I was the one who sat and organized the long pieces into crisscross patterns, much like a lattice piecrust, which made the matches more stable. Then, I dipped them into the harsh chemicals. Finally, I would hang the matches on clothespins and slide them through a large dryer. It was dangerous work. Many times, as we worked with groups of matches bundled together, fires would break out. Heat from the drying oven or even little sparks from the cutting process ignited the bundles. Many people suffered burns, myself included. Worse, I watched a few people catch completely on fire.

I started my day with twenty to thirty other factory workers at 8:00 a.m. We were supposed to stop work at 6:00 p.m., but oftentimes, we stayed until 10:00 p.m. Fourteen-hour days for a fourteen-year-old girl. They paid us slightly more for the overtime. In one month, I typically earned a few dollars in salary. During this time, this was considered "enough." I gave the little money I earned to my mother for groceries. Without the combined income from my sister and me, we would not have survived, so in that regard, I guess it was "enough."

4 | TEENAGER

When I turned fifteen, I started living with and working for the Buddhist lady who had attempted to raise me years earlier. I was no longer a flight risk. She needed someone to look after her home and do all the housework. In exchange, she promised to send me to school. Naturally, I thought it was a wonderful agreement. It turned out to be not much more than satisfactory. She fed me well and bought me nice clothes, but I never had the promised opportunity to go back to school. I did learn how to cook and keep a clean house. A year passed, and I told my mother I wanted to come home. I longed to be with my brothers and sisters. When one is used to being surrounded by many siblings, it's hard to be alone.

Back home again, I stuffed the blossoming, internal voices that whispered *you're unwanted* into the crevices of my heart. There was one kind of loneliness my siblings could not heal—the belief that I was replaceable. I hid my pain and kept moving forward. I was stubborn. It was also expected of me. No Korean child complains to her parents about feeling unloved.

One day, my daddy left for work—he still drove the truck—and had an accident. He ended up in jail for six months, and I cannot be sure of the reason. I suspect alcohol was involved. This put additional strain on our already fragile family. To compensate for the financial stress, I started working alongside my mom selling trinkets and food for cash. It was graduation season for the nearby schools, so we sold leis (much like in Hawaii) to teenagers, as they were customary for celebrations. I felt ashamed trying to hock these items to other girls my own age. I have never been a salesperson or extroverted in any way. I would have loved to keep to myself, but I was sixteen. I had to help support the family while daddy was in jail. Mother was doing whatever she could as well.

Our neighbor recommended we go to the train station in the early morning hours around 4:00 a.m. She explained we could buy items wholesale from incoming shipments and bring them to other parts of the city to sell. Each day, after we finished selling everything by 9:00 or 10:00 a.m., we bought fresh vegetables to trade on the street in the afternoons. I did everything I could to help my family while we waited for my daddy to be released.

One day, my mother sent me off again. This time, I went to a cousin's house (on her side of the family) to help her. She was pregnant at the age of thirty-six—considered older by medical standards at the time—and needed someone to keep her house, cook, and eventually, take care of her newborn daughter after her Cesarean section. She had lost her parents after the war, so she didn't have immediate family who could stay with her. The arrangement was for me to help my cousin and in return, her husband, who was a police officer, would help my daddy get out of jail sooner.

My already broken heart was crushed. It was always me who was sent away to work for others. I cried every night I was away. I wanted God to answer the question *Why me?* I didn't know the Lord yet, but

I later learned He knew me. He was there every time I was sent away, holding my tears and planning for my future. I know that now. During those times away, working for others, I learned so many things: how to cook, how to clean, how to care for a baby. I would use these skills later in my life.

I stayed with my cousin for nearly eight months. I took her daughter to the newborn medical check-ups. The clinic workers asked, "Are you the mother? You are too young to be a mother!" I was still only fifteen years old.

"No. I'm helping my cousin."

When my daddy had served his time and returned home, he promised he would do better. I believed him. A couple months later, he fell back into his old patterns. In fact, his drinking became worse. I felt so sad. I didn't want to deal with it anymore, so I left home with the bit of money I had saved up from all of my odd jobs. It was all I could think to do.

I searched everywhere and ultimately found a job in a restaurant. Back then, most restaurant employees lived inside the restaurants, so that's what I did. I worked during the day and shared a room and bathroom with several others at night.

On my own like this, I felt free. I made my own living. I had a place to lay my head, and I earned real money—and spent money—for the first time in my life. During one weekend, my new friends at the restaurant and I took a trip to the mountains. To prepare, I went to the marketplace and bought a pair of pants and a light blue striped shirt with a big collar. (It was the 1970's, after all!) I thought I was such a hotshot going up into the mountains with my friends, wearing the new clothes I had bought. For the first time, I was able to cut loose, have fun, and be a teenager for a bit.

***

A year passed, and I missed home again. I risked going back, hoping things would be different. I discovered nothing had changed. My daddy was still drinking, and the family still had no financial stability. Worse yet, inside those walls, I still did not feel wanted or cherished as a daughter should feel. Again, overwhelming sadness enveloped me. I don't remember crying. I just kept it all inside.

When the sadness wouldn't seem to ease, I made a decision that's hard to talk about. I spent a whole day wandering the city looking for every drugstore close to our home. I purchased whatever supply of sleeping pills—typically sold individually— I could find at each store. I shuffled home absorbed in the belief no one would miss me if I left this world. My death would not only mean one less mouth to feed; it would mean an end to the sadness. So I swallowed forty pills. I didn't think anything else about what I had done. I simply escaped to the attic— where all the girls slept in our house—and fell into bed, intent on taking my last nap on this earth. My final thought was *If I die, maybe it will straighten up my daddy so he'll care for the family*. I looked forward to being gone. I hoped my death would wake him up. I thought he might be a better daddy and husband. I never considered if the rest of my family would miss me. I couldn't understand a mother's love. I was not yet a mother, and my own mom had vacillated between protector, provider, and abandoner my entire life. I couldn't understand the depth of her love for me even though it was always there.

Many hours later, I woke up to the sound of my mother sobbing. In my drug-induced fogginess, I heard her say, "I don't care what we've gone through, these five kids are mine. I just want her to be alive." She was crying her heart out. She thought I was already dead.

My parents couldn't afford to take me to the hospital, so when I found consciousness, they called the local nurse who lived in the neighborhood. She came by to look at me. Since my blood pressure was rebounding, she told my parents I would live. I spent the next week vomiting up all the toxins in my body. I was so sick. I don't know how I woke up from my deep sleep except to say God was looking out for me before I ever knew Him. He had greater purpose in store for me.

This drastic call for help didn't change my daddy's ways. The very night I woke up to my mother's grief, he became drunk again. He was angry with me for what I had done. That night, I grasped a sobering truth: My actions had damaged my mother but changed nothing else. I realized there was nothing I could do to change my daddy. He was an addict through-and-through, and no amount of love, no level of crisis, and no impossible circumstance was going to break his heart enough to surrender control.

The shame I felt was heavy, weighing on me. I couldn't stay with my family anymore; I had disgraced them. I chose a day when everyone left, and I found myself alone in the house. I packed my bag and strode out the door. Like my mother had done a generation before me, I left home as a teenager, never to return.

PART II

DREAM HOME

"Put your outdoor work in order and
get your fields ready;
after that, build your house."
—Proverbs 24:27

5 | INDEPENDENCE

At age seventeen, I believed I was old enough to care for myself. My life of work and impromptu moves had afforded me the gifts of independence and street smarts. I knew I could live on my own. I wasn't scared. I did, however, verbalize the almost innate questions those who find themselves neck-deep in hardship tend to ask: *Why me? Why do I have to do this?* They were questions born from bitterness and hurt.

I knew from my past experience at the Korean restaurant that my best chance for survival was to work and live in another restaurant. A busy Chinese-American restaurant situated in the center of the city offered me that opportunity. As a new employee who chose to live in the restaurant, I secured a small corner of space on the open floor for my heavy blankets—a makeshift bed—and a few belongings. Six of us shared a single bathroom to clean up before work.

When nighttime gave way to dawn, we all packed up our blankets, mattresses, and cots and hid them away in a closet to make room for the tables the patrons would use when the restaurant opened. In Korea, people sat on the floor on pillows or mats to eat. We didn't use many chairs.

This environment may seem strange to some, but it wasn't to me at the time. Growing up in South Korea, many apartments, city dwellings, and farmhouses were built with one main room and a small, side kitchen area. The kids slept with the parents in that larger room. Someone would say, "Let's go to sleep," and everyone would line up on the floor and go to sleep at the same time. We kept warm by the charcoal-fueled pipes installed under the rock floor. In the morning, we cleaned up the evidence of bedtime and pulled out a table for eating.

Often, I was late waking up, so my family would simply push me to the side so they could start the day. I was a sleepy head because I lay awake at night while everyone else went to sleep when the lights went out. Once we ate breakfast, we'd pack up the table and food and make room for a living area to rest or play for the remainder of the day. There was nothing odd about the community living quarters at the restaurant when it was all I'd ever known at home.

When I turned eighteen, I changed restaurants and started working at one that was a neighbor to an American military base. It lay outside the city in a town called Uijeongbu, just north of Seoul. As U.S. servicemen frequented the restaurant, I watched with interest as friends and coworkers introduced themselves to these men, began dating, married, and then were whisked away to the States. I knew America was a different world than Korea. I'd also heard it was a better one. I remember thinking to myself, *well . . . this may be my only hope.*

I met a young fella. He was kind to me, but we couldn't communicate well. I knew no English, and he didn't speak Korean. After awhile, I was able to understand from him that we would never marry. He described himself as a single guy, but he didn't want to marry anyone—at least no one in Korea. Instead, he promised he would take care of me while he was stationed there, but when it was time, he would return to the States alone. I enjoyed his friendship and felt safe with him. He looked out for me, but sadly, he made due on the second part of his promise, as well. His turn to leave Korea came, and I never saw him again.

Dawn Caviness

The stories always seem to bubble up when I least expect it—while driving down the road, cleaning up the table after dinner, or while doing a mundane household task. Something in those moments will remind Suki of her past, and she will tell a small portion of her story. She doesn't make a habit of it. She rarely talks about herself. But occasionally, she will share a memory, a moment, or a snapshot of the past. And if I am not listening, I could miss it.

These moving stories have no grand introduction, illicit tears from her, nor do they hold any fanfare when shared. They are simply squeezed in-between the weather and talking about the grandkids. Suki remains stoic with very little emotion—factual, if you will.

But when I see them coming, I hold my breath and strain to hear the full story, the one behind her heavily accented English. As I do, I catch it—the magnitude of a life I cannot imagine—and I am nearly always moved to tears.

This moment was like many of the others. I was driving, and Suki sat next to me, looking out the window. The subject of love came up, and I asked the question: "Who was your first love?"

She paused and then told me the story of a G.I. she met in Korea. She said they were madly in love. She said she knew he not only loved her, but he really liked her. Sometimes, that's more important. He did things that showed how much he cared about her. When he saw how smart she was and how much she loved learning, he paid for her to take cosmetology classes at a local school in Korea. He also taught her how to "talk and act like a lady." She admitted that since she had worked as a waitress from the age of fourteen, she had picked up some abrasive language and an "attitude" from the other waitresses and American G.I.'s. No one had ever taken the time to tell her she could do better—be better—and that she was good enough to act and speak differently.

Suki sat next to me in that car and explained what they had as a couple was really special. But soon, it came time for him to go back to the U.S. He told her he couldn't take her with him. He didn't speak Korean perfectly, and she didn't speak English that well, but she said she understood perfectly. He said his family in America would not be open to accepting her. He explained, as best he could, he was going back to college, and he had a lot to learn and would be meeting lots of people—lots of other girls. He wasn't sure he was ready to marry. He just didn't think it could work.

She admitted that as he told her this, he cried. She knew he loved her, but she also knew he was right. He gave her his address and said if she ever came to the U.S., he would be there for her if she needed anything. As she finished the story, she looked back out the car window.

"What? Is that it? Do you still have his address? Did you find him?"

Despite the setbacks I had endured and the heartache I felt, I held fast to my two goals—buy my own house and get a formal education. I regarded the teenagers and young Korean women around me with envy. I wanted what they had which was the opportunity to learn in an official school setting. Since leaving school after the sixth grade, I had spent my learning years living on the run or working in factories and restaurants.

As I walked the streets of Seoul, I saw a disparity I could not ignore. On one side of the street stood a man of prosperity. He epitomized Seoul's shifting landscape from agricultural poverty to industrial wealth. He stood tall and was politely dressed. On the opposite side of the street sat a poor and downtrodden mother, her children tucked into her warmth, hoping to sell enough goods to pay for the food needed to satisfy their hungry bellies. It was clear which destiny I wanted, not just for myself but for any future family I might have.

As I looked for more work at a different restaurant, I lived in one of several rooms in a house owned by friends. My neighbors in the room down the hall liked to host parties. At their New Year's Eve party in 1974, I met a second serviceman from America. His name was William Anthony Caviness. People called him Anthony because his father was named Bill. He was a cute, young man. Others said he was good-looking. Anthony had dark hair and bright blue eyes. And he wasn't too tall.

My friend played matchmaker, and somehow it worked, even though I wasn't really impressed with this man. I compared him to the previous friend I had made who had treated me so well. These two men were just so different. The first one had grown up in a wealthy family outside Washington, D.C., and he knew how to treat women with respect. Anthony had grown up as a country boy in Randolph County, North Carolina. He wasn't as kind or polished, but I guess that didn't matter to me at the time.

After a few months, we were practically living together. He wanted to get married, but I didn't. The idea sounded good on the surface, but I knew we were such different people. It concerned me that we came from such different walks of life, and he was set in his ways. We fought about little, dumb things. I don't remember the details now. He picked on me, and I wanted him to be more mature. I had grown up so quickly (and much earlier) than most people, so I had trouble understanding his child-like ways. Perhaps my insecurity about my future and my need to feel loved drove me to stay in the relationship.

We were nineteen years old when Anthony wrote a letter to his mother explaining he had met someone in Korea whom he wanted to marry. She didn't want him to do it—to tie the knot. I felt like it was too easy to agree with her.

"See, your mother doesn't want you to get married."

I hoped it was enough to dissuade him. He was a rebel, though. He kept telling me we would get married, and he would take me to the States. So I simply said, "Okay."

I asked him if he had finished high school, and he said no. I told him he would need to do that if we were going to get married.

"You don't have an education. I don't have an education. How are we going to make a living in the States?"

After that conversation, he went to school for ten weeks in South Korea and received his high school diploma. He really wanted to marry me!

In April the following year, Anthony started the paperwork required for us to marry. He had to get approvals through the military, and I had to undergo background checks. He finalized everything in August, and I married Anthony on August 13, 1975. It all happened so fast. At first, I didn't even realize we were married. We were at the American embassy in Seoul when he pointed to a signature line on the bottom of the last page of a stack of papers. Without understanding the purpose of the papers, I did as he asked and signed them. He took them over to a window marked "Office of the Registrar." I stood in the middle of the lobby feeling conspicuous.

When he came back, he said, "That's it. We're married!"

I couldn't believe it. I stuffed my insecurities and said, "Well, that's it."

I thought, no matter what, I'm tied to him. I had somehow committed myself to this man and knew I'd be going to the United States. Looking back, I realize I chose this attitude with every surprising situation that had happened in my life. *It is what it is.* When difficult or unforeseen events came along I just put my head down, and I figured them out. There was no point in doing anything else.

Anthony told me his family was poor, but that didn't bother me. I had grown up living in tents for part of my life. I had panhandled on the streets of Seoul. I told him, "I don't care if we're poor. I just want to be able to work things out together."

I received my passport in September, and we saved up enough money to buy airplane tickets to North Carolina. I guess he wanted to make sure I wouldn't change my mind and run away, so he was intent on taking me to the States as soon as possible. He made sure I was going to be with him one way or another. The army granted him a leave in November, and we made our plans to travel to America.

My family came to the airport to say goodbye. That simple act of consideration and care shocked me. I assumed they would forget me. My mother was heartbroken to see me leave. As she cried at the gate, Anthony promised her, "I'll bring her back next year. Give me one year. I'll bring her back."

My new husband guided me with his hand on the small of my back so I would board the plane first. I think he was terrified my family would change my mind. I walked onto that giant airplane—Northwest Airlines it was. I remember it as if it was yesterday. I wondered how something so big could get off the ground. I didn't feel scared, but I was overwhelmed. The 747s had just started flying in Korea at the time, and to me, they were just big monsters. But they flew...

When the plane first took off in Korea, I gripped the armrests. I wondered if I'd ever return to my homeland. It was all I knew, but so many of my experiences were filled with pain, so I was also excited to be leaving for America. The mixed feelings made me jittery. I was starting a new life, and I hoped it would be a good one. I was surprised when I didn't feel much of the plane's movement while we were in the air. I thought, *How could this many people get off the ground at once?*

We landed in Tokyo first, followed by Hawaii. Then, we flew to Los Angeles and on to Chicago. Finally, we landed in Greensboro, North Carolina. Five flights. I wasn't sure if I'd be able to keep my eyes open for another minute. It was in the Greensboro airport where I learned Anthony had not told his mom and daddy we were coming home to visit. We took a taxi from the airport to his house in the country forty miles away. The car ride seemed unending. In Korea, we used trains for trips this long.

Once we left the Greensboro city limits, the only thing I saw was a thick blanket of trees on either side of the highway. Despite the daylight, dark woods stood everywhere I looked. *Where are we going? Where am I going to end up?*

When his mom saw the black car arrive in her driveway, she stepped out the front door. She told me later her first thought was the police had come to tell her that her son had gotten into trouble. She ran back into the house but willed herself to look out the door a second time. When we emerged from the taxi, she saw Anthony and ran out to hug and kiss him. Tears streamed down her face. He had been gone for a whole year, and a mother's relief shown in her smile. I stood there awkwardly thinking, *This is my new family.* Then, they turned to face me.

"Hello?" The word came out as a question rather than a statement. I felt the ends of my lips curl up with a mixture of hope and anxiety. I could not understand one word anyone spoke. I knew bits and pieces of English, but it was not enough to follow conversations, particularly ones laced with the country (Southern) accent. It was so hard to understand anything. His mother talked, and I just smiled.

My husband had repeatedly warned me his family was poor, but when I took in his family's home, it looked like pretty good living from my point of view. The Caviness family lived in an old, country farmhouse, but it had everything in it. It was a white, two-story home that sat in the middle of seven acres with a small pond in the back. They even owned their own cows. It was more comfortable than any place I had ever lived. I knew he was self-conscious of his family and their house, so I turned to him and said in the best English I could muster, "Well, it's okay!"

6 | ARMY WIFE

I loved Anthony's dad. When he returned home from work each day, I followed him around, hoping he would take the hint I wanted to go fishing again. Our trips to the streams, reservoirs, and ponds reminded me of living by the river in the Korean countryside. His dad and I caught fish, cleaned them, and cooked them together. He was the father figure I had missed out on as a young girl. He met my need for deep attention—willingly entered my world and cared about me. I'll never forget how I felt when I realized he enjoyed our time together as much as I did.

Anthony and I had been staying with his parents for one month when I learned I was pregnant. I couldn't ignore the morning sickness. Oh, I was so sick. I craved authentic Korean food like you can't know. This made me homesick. The Korean food available in North Carolina just wasn't the same.

Anthony still had a year of military service left. He was ordered to Fort Benning in Columbus, Georgia, so I went with him. I was thrilled to find some Korean restaurants and stores near the military base where we stayed. We didn't have the money to buy much of anything, but every once in a while, I went shopping and bought some authentic food from my home country. It was good for my soul.

My sister sent me letters during this time. She had grown in her faith, and she encouraged me to go to church in America. She even mailed me tapes of

Christian hymns, songs such as "Pass Me Not O Gentle Savior" and "Peace Like the River." The words still whisper to me in the stillness:

It is well with my soul,
it is well, it is well with my soul.

Without a phone in their home, I rarely spoke to my family except for major holidays. My family had to use their neighbor's phone to contact me. We all worried about the cost, so our conversations were short.

Finally, our son, Michael Anthony Caviness, was born in August 1976. It was one of the most glorious days of my life.

Dawn Caviness

In the car that day, when I asked Suki if she ever tried to find the G.I. she had loved, she laughed at my questions. Although she would never say it, I suspected she found my American response humorous since life, in most cases, is not like a Hollywood movie. She smiled and said, "No. I didn't ever try to find him, but I kept his address for a long time."

She shared that when he left, it was hard, but life went on. She had his address, and she kept it safe. Michael's dad and her became friends, and then they became more than friends, and before she knew it, she had fallen in love with him. They were married and moving to America—the place where her first love lived. So, instead of getting rid of the address, she kept it just in case she might need it. Just in case things didn't work out the way they were supposed to. Just in case she found herself alone. She loved Anthony and had no intention of looking for her ex-G.I. boyfriend, but life had taught her that nothing is guaranteed. So, she kept the address just in case.

She arrived to the United States, and life was incredibly hard shifting from Korean culture to the new culture of rural North Carolina. About a month later, she found out she was pregnant. Nine months later, she arrived home from the hospital with baby Michael in her arms.

A few days after she brought Michael home from the hospital, she realized her life was truly and forever changed. She went to where she had tucked away the G.I.'s address and pulled out the shriveled paper. She ripped it up into tiny pieces and threw it away. She said she knew, "This little baby, this family . . . they were my life now." No backup plan was needed. This plan had to work. This plan was going to work.

Suki looked back out my car's passenger window. Still, she gave away no emotions. I, on the other hand, couldn't control my tears. She glanced back at me and giggled. (She has the best giggle.) She always seems a bit surprised when her stories affect me in such a way. But this is the point of her stories—the happy ending. Each of her stories ends with a phrase or sentiment of, "Don't be sad; it all worked out in the end." She puts a beautiful bow on top of a heap of hurt others would try to hide. She talks about how God used her life story to bring her to Him, how throughout this long story of her journey to the U.S, working in a mill, and raising her children, God was coming for her and calling her through it all.

When she finishes her stories with how God took her circumstance and did something great with them, that's when she cries. The strongest woman I have ever known becomes full of emotion. When she talks about God's love and how she has found worthiness in Him, tears well up in her eyes, and her usually steady voice cracks. Although she talks about the rest of her story as historical fact, of "what was," she is moved to her core when it comes to the love of God.

The post-war love story between her and a long-lost G.I. is just that to her—a story, a part of her past. She isn't sad about what could have been. She has no regrets. What moves her, what provokes emotion, and where the end of her story always lands is on the deep, unconditional love she has found in God. A true love, one that has never let her down, despite the long, hard journey.

A year went by, and I looked forward to settling down with our new family of three as Anthony's time in the army came to a close. However, Anthony made the unexpected decision to re-enlist— re-up, as I learned to say. The army gave him a choice about where he wanted to serve. He put in for Korea and was granted his wish. So when Michael was six months old, we left North Carolina and returned to South Korea. It was February 1977.

Anthony had promised my mother when we left Korea he would bring me back. He was making due on his promise. I was grateful. He wanted me to be happy, and I was. The problem was because my family had never owned a telephone, I had sent a letter to them explaining we were returning and gave them a tentative week of our arrival. Once it was time to travel, I didn't know where to find them. My parents had lost their home again, and I didn't know where they were living. I wasn't even sure they had received my last letter. Once we arrived in Seoul, my plan was to find local merchants who were familiar enough with my family to know where they were living.

By God's Providence, our taxi from the airport toward the area of town where my parents used to live almost hit a pedestrian. When I looked up and out the window to see what had happened, I saw my mother on the other side of the street! I jumped out of the taxi to greet her. When she realized it was me, she cried tears of joy and wrapped me in a full-size hug. It was not unlike Anthony's reunion with his mother back in North Carolina several months before. My heart was full.

My family was renting a tiny house with two rooms on the hillside. My parents and brothers shared one room, and my oldest sister and her family (she was married and had a child at this point) stayed in the other room. My younger sister was working and living in a restaurant, following in my footsteps I guess.

Anthony was so sweet. He told me we would try to help them as much as we could while we were in Korea. We lived in the village near base. I was able to spend time with my family, tell them what America was like—I mentioned the vast number of trees—and tried to explain how my life would look when Anthony was finished with military life. We couldn't help my family as much as I wanted to financially since we were living on a serviceman's salary, but I tried to paint a picture of prosperity in America. I dreamed about the day when my whole family might live without the fear of being hungry again. I secretly hoped they would move to America with me.

During that year in Korea, in 1977, my daddy passed away. He suffered a stroke and died the first week in April. I was so grateful to be there—even for just the few months beforehand—to spend time with him before he passed. I was sad for my brothers. They were still young—ten and thirteen years old at the time—but I felt something close to relief for everyone else. He had become a burden with his struggles with alcoholism and then the stroke. My mother and sister were tasked with caring for him, so his death a few days after the stroke was not a terrible thing. I was also able to help my mom with the funeral arrangements. Anthony stayed on base, and I attended the services with my family.

Anthony and I returned to the States in 1978. This time, we landed at Fort Gordon in Grovetown, Georgia near Augusta. All this time, Anthony made me feel special. I was the mother of his child, and he had requested to be stationed in Korea so we could be close to my family for a year. He let me make more decisions, manage our budget, and buy the things I needed to care for Michael.

We were still broke, but Anthony wanted to make sure we weren't missing out on certain necessities, so we went ahead and bought what we could—a car, washer and dryer, and some furniture. While in Fort Benning, we had rented all these things from the military. Now at Fort Gordon, Anthony wanted us to own them ourselves.

After making our monthly payments on all our purchases, we had hardly a dime left over. It was hard. I wanted to work, but Anthony said no. I don't believe he want me to be "Americanized." Anthony harbored the ridiculous idea that he could bring a Korean wife to the United States, but the American culture and the people around me shouldn't affect me. My own dreams didn't matter to him. He assumed I would always be a good, sweet, stay-at-home mother, taking care of the children and the house.

I was (and still am) very independent. I didn't like relying on a man for security. I had spent my entire life working. It was all I knew, and I wanted that piece of mind, financial security, and freedom. So I ignored his wishes and started working a minimum-wage job in a cookie factory in Augusta, Georgia. Murrays Cookies (and Biscuit Company) made vanilla wafers, and unbeknownst to me at the time, would go on to become part of the Keebler empire in 1998.

In the late 1970's, I started packing the cookies and then moved on to the job of cutting the cookies. There were quite a few Korean ladies working there. Word of mouth is a powerful tool. I had found a Korean community, and we frequently shared job information and memories of our homeland. We were known in the factory for our hard work, so they continued to hire Koreans from our community.

After transportation and babysitting costs, the money I kept didn't amount to much. Yet it allowed me to push back against Anthony's idea of keeping me dependent on him. I succeeded in securing my driver's license to cut down on the transportation costs. I worked second shift at the factory, so I asked Anthony to watch Michael during the evenings until I came home. Since he was at the army base, he had some flexibility. I did this so we wouldn't have to pay so much for a sitter. With each passing month, I stole back more and more independence, all while saving a tiny bit of my own money.

"I want to work so I can help my family back in Korea."

I was raised in a culture that supports family, more so than in the United States I believe. Family honor and support were engrained in me from the time I was selling vegetables on the streets of Seoul. I didn't want to forget his parents either.

"I want to be able to help your parents, too."

If I wasn't working at the cookie factory, I was helping his family in some way.

***

We lived in Georgia for two-and-a-half years, and Anthony came to me one day to say he wanted to go back to Korea. He had not left the military yet, despite his promises to do so. I was afraid if he put in for Korea, he might get stationed in Germany. He ignored my advice, and sure enough when he requested South Korea, he was assigned to Germany. He was so stubborn.

In order to avoid the assignment, Anthony went to jump school (skydiving school). After completion, he had nine months left in the service. The army sent him to Newport News, Virginia—Fort Eustis. I was nine months pregnant, so I told him I wasn't going with him. I wanted to stay with his parents and have our baby, but he wouldn't agree to that plan. I relented, as I often did, and packed up my things. I was so uncomfortable riding in that pick-up truck from North Carolina to Virginia with a baby itching to come out. That same month, on February 27, 1980, I had our second child, Robert Ashley Caviness.

When Anthony's last nine months were up, he left the service after seven years. Of course after all this time, I realized there were benefits for us if he was in the military—a consistent paycheck and healthcare to name a couple of those perks.

"If you stay in the service thirteen more years, I'll follow you anywhere you go, and I might even have more children."

I harbored fear about our financial stability, so I was willing to be the housewife he wanted for a few more years.

"No."

It was all he said. He didn't want to stay in the service; he was fed up, so he got out.

"Once you get out, I'm going to make a home with my boys. I'm going to get a job, and I'm going to buy myself a house. A real home."

I wanted to give my boys a safe place to call their own. I was finished with tents, the constant moving around, and the feeling of insecurity. I had known those things all my life, and it's not what I wanted for my boys. So we went back to Randolph County, North Carolina and lived with my in-laws for two years, and I feverishly saved money.

My mother-in-law worked at a mill. She had already spoken with the "boss man" and told him I would make a great employee. They brought me in, and I had a job before the week was over. Actually, both Anthony and I had gone and interviewed at the mill, and we were both offered jobs.

I said to him, "Is this really what you want to do? I think you need to find something better." I assumed he would have more opportunities than me since he had finished high school in South Korea, so he agreed.

The funny thing was that as quickly as Anthony left the service, he wanted to return to military life so badly. He didn't like the job of looking for a job. It was hard, probably because he couldn't get situated anywhere. He would find work and do it for a bit, but then he'd leave to find something else. He'd work for a little bit more at another odd job, and then he'd leave again. He kept moving around, never settling on one idea or workplace. I couldn't depend on him.

While he jumped from one thing to another, I worked at the mill, and my in-laws helped with childcare. A couple years later, I finally convinced him to come back to the mill with me. We needed the money. He agreed, and he actually stayed put for two-and-a-half years.

Michael Caviness

When I think of my mom, my first thoughts steer towards her humbleness, hardworking attitude, and selflessness. Her humility may be absent from a lot of her stories in this memoir because she's not going to share that part of her with you. That's how humility works—it's living life with your lens focused on others above yourself.

My mom had an incredible reputation wherever she went. She worked in a textile mill for over twenty-five years and was often praised for being the hardest worker there. It reached the point where many of her coworkers didn't like her because her productivity made them look bad. My mother's supervisors often pointed to my mom's work ethic as the standard that other employees should meet. I know all this because I worked in the same mill with her for six years. I was able to see my mom from a different perspective. I was able to see just how good she was at serving, working, and doing her best in everything she touched. I felt both humbled and proud when I discovered all the vice presidents, and even the mill owner, knew her because of her hard work. It was an honor to walk around the mill and be called "Suki's kid."

During all the time spent in the military and with all the moves we made, I visited church a few times. The Korean community gathered in the local church, so that's where I went to be with other Koreans. I mostly attended with our neighbors, who were Christians. Every time I went to church, I felt jittery. Every time I prayed, I felt funny. I confessed to my neighbor friend that my whole body would get fidgety at church.

She smiled. "Some day, if you stay in the church, you will see the mercy of God."

That's what she told me. I didn't believe anything at the time. I didn't know Jesus on a personal level. I was just going for the fellowship and to spend time with other people like me. It was a social fix. Her words stayed with me for a long while, though.

After some time passed at the mill, Anthony decided to pursue one of his post-military benefits—education. He took a layoff package and started school to become an electrician. While he was in school and I was at the mill, my in-laws continued to help us with babysitting the boys, who were now seven and three years old.

My in-laws and I got along just fine. My mother had taught me that once I married someone, I was part of that new family. I was taught to be respectful and kind to my husband's parents and obey them. That is the Korean way. I tried to do as much as I could to help them but I was busy, too—cleaning the house, working second shift, and running kids where they needed to be. I was in constant motion from sun-up to about midnight every day. I continued to put money away, a little at a time into the local credit union. I wanted to buy my own home so bad. That dream had not died.

7 | MY LITTLE HOUSE

In 1982, I earned my United States Citizenship with the help of my friends and neighbors. They read U.S. history to me, showed me a map of all the states, taught me about civics, and questioned me until I knew the information well enough to pass the exam. I thought if nothing else, even if I never had my own home, at least I'd have this.

With citizenship, the government permitted me to invite my family to live here with permanent residence green cards. It was a huge opportunity for my brothers. If they were willing to work, they could make a good living in America and do well. That was one of the biggest differences between South Korea and the U.S. at that time—opportunity. I reached out to invite my mother and brothers to America. I didn't get an answer from my family right away.

Anthony and I bought a trailer and put it next to his parent's house on their land in 1983. What family doesn't want its own space? We lived there for two years, and I kept saving money. The trailer was a good first step, but I knew eventually I wanted that real home I had been dreaming about for so long.

About that time, I received word my mother was sick. She was having heart problems related to her childhood battle with rheumatic fever. I was worried I wouldn't get to see her again, that soon she'd be gone. With each passing day, my fear grew and gave birth to sorrow. I had two kids, a husband to care for, and monthly payments to make. I didn't have enough money to send back to my family in Korea or use for travel to help with her care. Depression entered my world for the second time in my life.

My co-workers at the mill tried to encourage me. "You live in a trailer, but you have a roof over your head," they told me. "You're doing okay. You don't need to buy a house. You need to go see your mother." I had been relentless in my pursuit to buy a house and had saved about three thousand dollars by this point. My friends convinced me to use that money and go home to my mom. As I said, in Korean culture, family comes first.

I left Michael and Robert—still seven and three—with my in-laws and travelled alone to South Korea. My mother was in better condition than I expected. She didn't need much care. My brothers had grown. One was in college, the other in high school. I asked them again if they wanted to return to America with me. They decided not to leave Korea since Mother wanted them to finish school first. My oldest sister and her family decided to stay put for the time being, as well. My heart was broken. I had such high hopes for returning with someone from my family. I told myself, in typical fashion, that it was okay, and I flew (on the still monstrous 747) back to North Carolina alone.

In 1984, Anthony finished his schooling and found a job as an electrician. Finally, we were both working. Better than that—it hadn't taken long with his income to put away enough money in that credit union account for a down payment on a house. I was more than ready to find that little home of my dreams for my boys and me.

I was a happy woman at this point. My boys were content, healthy, and growing. My husband had a job. And we had some money. The only hiccup with buying a house was the interest rate for home purchases. In 1984, it was twelve percent! I decided it didn't matter, and we started house hunting. While touring one home, I happened to look farther down a little hill and saw the house of my dreams. It was a brown brick-front home with a carport, red roof, paved driveway, and flat yard. It was cute. It wasn't for sale at the time, but God was about to intervene on our behalf.

A few weeks later, it, too, miraculously went on the market. We bought it. You couldn't have erased the smile from my face if you had tried. My own home! My name was on the mortgage. A lifetime dream thirty years in the making had just become reality. I giggled the days away. I thought back to the river in the Korean countryside next to our tent city where my sister and I had built our makeshift house from rocks and dreamed of our futures. I wondered what she would think of my new home.

The following year, my mother decided she wanted to come live in the United States. My younger brother had finished high school, and all my talk about The American Dream had convinced her there were more opportunities in the States. She didn't want my brothers to take just any jobs they could find in Korea. She wanted them to thrive. I started the paperwork to get her over here first. U.S. Immigration automatically approved her to move here. Legally, she was permitted to bring her two sons over eighteen months later. If I had tried to bring my brothers over myself, it would have taken four or five years. It was just the way the process worked.

My mother moved into my new, little house in September 1985. Her reaction to my house satisfied a deep longing of mine.

"You've got a pretty place here for your family." It was her way of telling me she was proud of me.

But she stayed for only two weeks. She watched how hard I worked to make our monthly payments, and she didn't want to be in the way. At least, that's what she told me. My first cousin lived in New York and needed childcare for her two young children. My mom decided to move there to help my cousin and earn some money. Even though she was only in her fifties, she didn't want to work in the mill with me. She thought it was too difficult.

"I can go to New York and babysit. I'll stay there for a year or two until your brothers are able to come over. We'll have enough money to send them for plane tickets."

With that, she left. My heart broke yet again. After years of prodding and begging, my mother had finally moved to the States, and after two short weeks, she left me again. I knew she was right; childcare was a much easier job than what I was doing at the mill. I rationalized away my pain and fell back on my old mantra. *It is what it is.*

My cousin forwarded me Mom's money each month. She sent six hundred dollars the first month, seven hundred dollars the third month, and nine hundred dollars by the fifth month. I deposited her money in a bank account in North Carolina because my mom didn't know how to handle money. In order for her to bring my brothers over, we not only had to be employed, but we had to show we had the economic means to support them until they found jobs of their own. There were many legal hoops to navigate, and word on the street was the government really did check these things.

My mother stayed in New York for eighteen months, and ultimately my brothers arrived from Korea in February 1987. They came directly to my house since that was the address on all the immigration paperwork.

When they arrived from the airport and entered my house through the carport, they first saw the wood heater, which was directly across the living room. I had the fire burning since it was wintertime. They really thought it was something! They were used to city life in South Korea, and this little house in the country was different, to say the least. They kept asking each other, "This is Sister's house?" I was proud of myself for making my dreams a reality.

I arranged for their social security cards and driver's licenses and was able to get all of that done in a week. I was busy, busy, busy—still working twelve-hour shifts. My brothers only stayed with me for that first week. Then, they decided to head to New York to be with our mother.

About this time, Anthony's and my marriage was in turmoil. He had never said ugly things to me before, but for some reason, he started throwing everything back in my face. He pointed out every mistake I made and blamed me for everything that went wrong. He was so mean to me—verbally abusive some might have called it. On one particular day, he was so unkind to me while I was making a casserole that I threw the baking dish down in the sink, and it broke into hundreds of pieces. As the glass flew everywhere, my hands were cut and started to bleed. It was scary. I wrapped them up in the bathroom, but our frustration with each other couldn't be mended. On that day, Anthony discovered his wife wasn't going to relent; I would fight back.

After the day I bled all over my broken dish, I decided I couldn't live with the unkindness any longer. I knew I couldn't just leave Anthony, though. I knew I had to work it out with him, try to change things. So I went to counseling. After some time, we even went to counseling together. One of the cracks in our relationship was that Anthony enjoyed sitting around the house watching television. He was a homebody. I couldn't be more different. I enjoyed traveling and experiencing new adventures. My country heart longed for the great outdoors. Fishing was one of my favorite hobbies, ignited by my time with his father years before.

Our counselor recommended a date day— make peanut butter sandwiches and have a picnic in the park. She knew we didn't have much money, so she had suggested something simple. We never went to the park. Anthony brushed it off as a silly idea.

She continued to encourage Anthony to spend more time with me, doing things outside the house. He was working night shift, I was working twelve-hours days, our two children had ball games . . . we just didn't have any empty space on the calendar for each other. Our hands were full.

On one occasion, we were able to go to the beach together. His parents had taken the kids down early, and we drove down together after work on

Friday. We spoke maybe two words the whole three-hour drive. He was checked-out. When we arrived at the beach, he spent much of the time sleeping. I figured he would get over whatever was wrong sooner or later.

***

In 1987, my full plate became heavier when my mother and brothers moved back to North Carolina from New York. The first thing my brothers wanted to do when they moved to North Carolina was find a church. I felt a small measure of shame when I couldn't tell them where the nearest (or any) Korean church was located. I could only think to take them to the army base. I knew there were many Koreans living there—members of military families. I assumed there was a Korean church nearby, and maybe someone could point us in the right direction. My brothers ended up finding a church and attended regularly, even though it was in Fayetteville, a two-hour drive away.

During this time, I asked Anthony, "Will you help me get through the next six to twelve months? I just want to get my family settled and find them jobs." He simply nodded. I confided in my mother that I just couldn't do it anymore, be married to someone so unkind. She told me I had no choice. I called for a truce.

"He married you. You can't leave the person who brought you here. You have to love him the way he is. You can't just give up like that."

It was the Korean way.

My brothers could see the pain my marriage caused me. My older brother said, "Suki, Sister, just forget about it and go to church with us."

I will never forget my response.

"I would love to go to church. But if I go to church every Sunday with you, Anthony will run me off. I don't think it's going to work." So, I didn't go to church with my family, and I stayed with Anthony.

My brothers returned to New York for two weeks because they thought they could find jobs more easily. They were having little luck in North Carolina. My cousin helped them look around, and they did find some odd jobs, but nothing that would afford them any real life. They were living in a Korean neighborhood.

One day, my brother called me. "Sister, if you can give us a room and help us find a job, we'll come back down. I came here to live the American life, not the Korean life." He asked me to help him learn English. He wanted to do everything the American way.

A couple months later, my mother and brothers were living in a little apartment in Ramseur, North Carolina close to our house. My older brother found a job in the same mill where I worked. My other brother found a job in a different mill. My mom was getting bored with staying at home in the apartment by herself, so she asked me to take her somewhere to get a job. Off to the employment office we all went.

The lady we met with said, "Well, she can't speak English, but she can work somewhere. A Korean woman owns a dry cleaning business down the road a bit. I don't know if they're hiring, but you can go check it out."

My mom, brothers, and I looked at each other and said, "What do we have to lose?" So we stopped by the dry cleaners.

As soon as we walked in, a little, bitty lady walked up from the back. Her face lit up when she saw "family" standing there. After explaining our presence, it turned out she wanted my older brother to work for her, not my mother.

We continued talking, and she said she was the wife of a Korean Methodist minister, and their church wasn't far from their business. We couldn't believe our ears. My brothers had still been seeking a closer church to call home. Our meeting this Korean woman was the first time in my life when I realized God leads His people to the places they need to be.

When my family met the Methodist preacher for the first time, he promised them, "If your family comes to our church, I'm going to teach you how to catch the fish instead of feeding you the fish." My brothers and mother immediately started attending the Korean United Methodist Church. It was June. In September, they all moved to Asheboro, North Carolina to be even closer to my brother's new job and the church. My brother continued to invite me to join them for the Sunday services. I continued to decline.

I knew their move to Asheboro would be the end of me helping my family search for jobs, places to live, and a church. It was obvious they had found a community to collectively call home, and they were no longer dependent on me. Part of me felt the weight of all that responsibility lift from my heart and mind.

After all, it was me who had convinced them to leave Korea for a better life, so I wanted to make sure they found it. I was also thankful I could help them move forward and get settled in America.

Anthony must have been waiting for the right moment. Once my family was settled and had secure jobs, he came to me with some news I wasn't expecting. It left me stunned.

8 | HEARTBREAK

"**I** can't live with you anymore. I'm moving out. I'm going to live at my mother's house."

It was October, and Anthony's sudden confession punched me square in the gut. It was so out of the blue. I assumed we were going to work everything out. We had been to counseling. He had supported my desires to help my family. I did not expect this at all. I had stayed with him even when I had been ready to move out numerous times in the past to escape his cruelty. It didn't seem fair.

With his words, the sum of my entire life's disappointments flooded back into the present—my mother's rejection when she sent me off with my dad back to Busan. My dad's rejection when I had swallowed all those pills. My family's rejection when they forced me to move out to live with and work for other people. I found a few words among the jumble of emotions poised to suffocate me.

"When are you going to move out?" They were irrational words to me at the time, because I honestly didn't believe he meant what he said.

"Three days. On Saturday."

"You really want to move out?"

"Yes."

Those three days went by in a blur as I battled shock and disbelief. I kept thinking he would change his mind or that he was exaggerating, threatening something he wouldn't really carry out. To say I was devastated would be a gross misuse of the English vocabulary. I was more than devastated. I wondered how he could do this to our kids. He may not have been a good husband, but he was a good daddy. They needed him.

The weekend arrived, and I was scheduled to work. I left for the mill and wondered what would happen. About mid-day, my neighbor called me at work.

"Anthony is moving everything out of your house. I think you should be here."

I couldn't leave work. After my shift, I returned to a much emptier house. We didn't have many belongings to begin with, but he had taken what he believed to be his, which was most of everything. I went numb.

On Sunday, the first thought that filled my mind when I opened my eyes to an empty bed was I needed to go to church. More thoughts flooded my head:

Yes, now I can go to church.
I want to keep the rest of my family together.
I want to raise my two boys in the church.
What do I have to lose?

I wonder if these were not my thoughts but the whispers of my Heavenly Father above. I had Sundays off from work, so we started going to the Korean United Methodist Church where my family attended. Michael was eleven years old, Robert seven.

The kids didn't understand why their daddy had moved out. I didn't have any explanations to give them. They could see me struggling. My heart broke for them but not for myself. I am not sure I still loved Anthony at that point. Maybe I never had. I just wanted to rescue my kids from the wreckage. I didn't want their lives to be emotionally handicapped because their father abandoned us.

The Korean culture is a private one, and my own experiences had formed a wall around my heart. I had learned early on that people don't share their feelings, particularly negative ones. It's why writing this memoir is so difficult. But my love for my boys and my need to protect them from the same type of pain I had as a child was important to me. I wanted us to grieve together.

My mother was shocked, too. She couldn't function. She blamed herself for our broken marriage. I tried to assure her it was not her fault.

During one of his visits with Michael and Robert, Anthony told them something that catapulted me from shock and sadness to rage.

"It was because the Koreans moved in I can't live there no more."

When I found out he said this to Michael and Robert, my insides simmered. I didn't want the boys to be forced into picking a side, but it seemed that was what Anthony was doing. His unfair tug-of-war spurred me to reassess my own parenting philosophy. I would not put my kids through the Korean Way where emotions were bottled up, affection was limited, and financial instability was common. I decided to raise them the American Way. From that point forward, I never forced them to eat Korean food or hold Korean traditions, though I still did. The only part of the culture I wanted them to live out was love for family and respect for everybody.

Those around me asked me if I would return to Korea when my marriage ended.

"No, no. My children are Americans," I responded. My boys were my highest priority, and I wanted to make sure they received a good education. I knew America was where they needed to be.

Anthony wanted custody of the boys. His intentions were for me to give up the kids and let his parents raise them. That was ridiculous. I was a more strong-willed and independent woman than he realized. I wouldn't let go of them. We had some ugly conversations between us, but my sole purpose in life was to keep my boys. I believe God was on my side.

I struggled for about ten months after the separation. I had custody of Michael and Robert— Praise the Lord—and I was attending Korean church and working. However, finances were a real problem. I cut corners wherever I could. I didn't know how I was going to keep the house, the children, and my sanity.

Michael Caviness

My dad had always handled paying the bills and balancing the checkbook because my mom didn't know English very well. Shortly after he left, I watched as my mom sat at the kitchen table and copied every number from one to one hundred, all the hundreds, and each thousand, spelled out in words, onto a piece of notebook paper she tucked into her checkbook. She knew she had to learn how to write checks on her own to pay the bills, and she took the painstaking initiative to teach herself with some help from me. At the time, I don't think I understood why she was doing what she was doing.

She hid that list of numbers in her wallet for years. I can't be sure, but she may still keep it with her.

A painful memory for me is when my mom asked Robert and me if we would be willing to go on the Free Lunch Program because she didn't think she could afford lunches anymore. We easily qualified. We begged her not to put us on the program because everyone at school knew who those kids were. Our youthful pride prevented us from helping Mom out. She pulled out a twenty-dollar bill and said, "This is all we have to live on for the next week and a half."

But she didn't make us do it. She didn't want us to be embarrassed, so somehow she made it work. If I had to guess, I'd say she went without lunch (or made a similar sacrifice) to avoid having us feel embarrassed about the Free Lunch Program. Our naïveté and childish reaction to the Free Lunch Program still haunts Robert and me to this day.

My friend, Jennifer, introduced me to her pastor. She knew I needed help. Pastor Terry became a mediator between Anthony, his family, and me. My relationship with his parents had soured. This, too, broke my heart. His mother had been watching the kids for a couple hours after school until I could get home from work. When Anthony left, she wanted one hundred dollars instead of fifty dollars. There were nasty words between us, but I know many of mine were misunderstood. I wanted them to know how I felt, but my anger and pain prevented me from communicating well. If I had the money, I would have given it to her, but I was financially stretched. After a few comments from Anthony's mother about raising the boys herself, I feared she and his dad would just take Michael and Robert from me. At that point, I cursed her, and I hid my boys with another sitter after school so she couldn't take them away. Every action I took and word I spoke was done from a place of fear.

I wanted Anthony's parents to love their grandchildren unconditionally, not because I paid them to care for them. I knew we were hurting one another with our words, and my anxiety about losing my children was suffocating me. I invited Anthony and his parents to meet at their house with Pastor Terry and myself. He was an unbiased intercessor, able to speak truth and hope into our brokenness. His guidance and God's grace moved mountains, and after our meeting, I felt comfortable leaving the boys with Anthony's mother again.

Robert Caviness

After Dad left, I knew we struggled financially, but I was young and prideful. I feel terrible about it now, thinking of ways that we could have helped, but Mom always found a way to provide everything we needed. Not long after my dad left, she bought my brother and me our first pair of Nike shoes. It was practically all we received for Christmas—besides some socks and underwear—but we were so excited to have our first pair of name-brand shoes. She had worked hard to see the smiles on our faces. Michael and I always knew that Mom's love was without fail.

Some time after my separation, my brother became sick. My mom was also ill with heart problems. The kids had so much going on in school, and it was all too much to handle. I was about to lose myself. I feared going crazy. There was a perpetual knot in my chest. My hands often trembled, and depression entered my world for the third time, partnering with my anxiety like a conjoined twin. I felt trapped by all my circumstances.

One day in the middle of the chaos, as I drove back from the hospital after a visit with my brother, my emotions—which had been bottled up for too long—begged for release. I banged my fist on the steering wheel and shouted, "I can't do this anymore!"

Without thinking, I opened my hand and lifted it skyward. "There is Jesus! I will turn to Him! I can restart with Him!"

That day in the car, I promised God and myself, "God, if You take my burdens away, I will follow You for my whole life. I don't know You that well yet, but God, I will follow You." It was an ultimatum, but it was born from a place of dependence on Him—from total surrender. And God responded.

The knot gripping my heart loosened. It was the most peaceful feeling I'd ever experienced in my whole life. All the anger about my circumstances, Anthony's abandonment, and my childhood rejections melted away. The bitterness disappeared. My fear eased. Indescribably, I smiled. In the time it took to call out His name, I suddenly saw and felt God in an entirely new way. I knew His forgiveness. It was as real as my two boys. As real as the steering wheel in front of me.

My situation hadn't changed at all. I was at the bottom of a deep ravine of financial stress and emotional chaos, but that didn't seem to matter anymore. God introduced me to joy that day. It was a joy removed from all that was going on in my life.

Instead of heartbreak and sorrow, I felt gratitude. I felt His redemption evaporate my anger like cool drops of rain on hot pavement. I started counting my blessings—all the ways God had shown up and loved me through the years. I could see them clearly.

_____

I have my health.
I have my two sons.
I have a roof over my head.
I have a job.
I have my family here.
I have a church to go to.

_____

God is so good.

PART III

ETERNAL HOME

"Therefore you are no longer strangers
and foreigners, but fellow citizens of
the saints and members of God's
household."
—Ephesians 2:19

9 | SINGLE MOTHER

M y acceptance of Jesus as my Savior was a true conversion. If there was ever a before and after poster child for Christianity, I was it. I couldn't stop grinning with this new joy I had discovered. People at work asked me, "Why do you keep smiling throughout the day?" We worked in a mill after all. They didn't understand. They assumed I had found a new boyfriend. I told them I did find someone, and His name was Jesus.

I saw people differently too. I mean I really saw them. Before, I couldn't look people directly in the eyes. Partly the Korean Way, and partly my inability to understand my self-worth, I gazed downward when interacting with others who I felt held more authority—parents, bosses, teachers . . . men. After surrendering to God, I discovered I was able to look people in the eye. And I saw them as loved by Him. I knew He loved me too.

Even though I had found joy, Michael and Robert were kids and they complained. They didn't want to go to the Korean church anymore. We left home at nine o'clock in the morning and typically didn't get home until three o'clock in the afternoon. When church ended, we traipsed through the Korean store for a bit. It was late in the day before we made our way back home where they finally had free time. After nine months of this routine, the kids professed, "This is not for us."

Ever since the second grade, classmates had ridiculed Michael and Robert for being Asian. They made fun of what the kids only knew to call their "Chinese eyes." I spoke with their teachers about this often, but I couldn't speak the "right" language. Conveying my heart was still difficult for me, let alone using English to do so.

Now I know differently, but I believed Michael and Robert grew up listening to my broken English, and that was the reason they had not learned to speak correctly themselves. Both received speech therapy in school. Because of all this, I harbored feelings of guilt for being "different." It was agony for me when I first realized our cultural distinctions caused my boys to feel so conspicuous. When Anthony left us, my biggest fear was failing my boys because I didn't have an education, couldn't write, couldn't speak fluent English, and looked different than almost everyone around us. Despite the community we had found, going to the Korean church was too much for my boys to handle, so we stopped attending.

Through all my insecurities and their peers picking on them, Michael and Robert never denied who I was or from where I had come. At each of their ball games and when they performed in their band performances, I was there. I'm sure the people around them referred to me as their "Asian" mother, but my boys never rejected me. I knew some parents in the Asian community who made it a point to avoid the public eye. Their kids asked them to, so they relinquished that part of parenthood. When my boys didn't ask that of me, it gave me the strength to go on. I hope they know how much that meant to me. God was looking after their hearts, and they were looking after mine.

I knew God had purpose in gifting me with my two boys. I wanted to keep them in church somewhere. Nine months before this, my friend, Jennifer, had introduced me to her pastor at a Wesleyan church who ended up mediating my relationship with Anthony's parents after our split. Unbeknownst to me during that time, God was lining up something (really, Someone) for me to run to in my hour of need.

It was 1988. I nervously called Pastor Terry.

"I don't know anything about your American church, but I know God has given me this peaceful mind. I believe He has saved me. Will you take my boys and me into your church?"

"Of course we will."

It was an old church that housed wooden pews with creamy blue cushions and stained glass windows on the lateral walls. Pastor Terry told me he used to work in a large church in Chicago where Asians attended, and he knew a little something about our culture. He and his wife took us into their arms. I was the only Korean in a sea of white people. It didn't matter; everyone there welcomed us with open arms just as their pastor and his wife had. They even affirmed me as a parent, something I desperately needed at the time.

"Your boys are so polite."

I tried to learn all the faces and names, each one an angel to me. Since I worked every other Sunday, one of these angels picked up my boys on those Sundays I couldn't attend so they could go to church even when I wasn't able to go. That meant the world to me. The congregation stood by me as I navigated this new season of life as a single mother. I felt included like never before. For a woman who struggled to feel accepted by her own family as a child, it was remarkable to be so accepted by others.

On the Sundays I could attend, I found myself drawn to the altar. I couldn't help but cry out to God, praise Him, and give Him His due glory.

I didn't know how to read the Bible, but I knew the Spirit of God was sustaining me from the inside out. Pastor Terry was thankful I was there to grow in my faith. I learned how to read English by singing in church. My first finger slid across each word in the hymnal as I memorized it. It wasn't long before I was baptized. Michael and Robert were baptized alongside me—the greatest gift for a believing mother. The pastor was such a good shepherd to my boys and me.

I learned so much from Pastor Terry's teachings. I was soaking it all in and soon started reading The New Testament on my own. Everything took on a whole new meaning. Or maybe I just had a whole new understanding of what had already happened inside me. And after a time, Pastor Terry invited me to give my testimony.

God continued to mold my heart. Not long after we started to attend the Wesleyan church, I went back and apologized to Anthony's mother for all the things I had said in fear after our separation. She apologized to me, too. It was a beautiful reconciliation.

"How did I make a living all these years without God?" I wondered, sometimes out loud. I was thirty-three years old. I had no idea how I had survived through all my struggles without Him. As I read the Bible, I realized God had, in truth, always been with me. I just hadn't been able to see His presence yet. I vowed to make Jesus my rock—to stick with Him. I fell from that rock from time to time, but I never lost that peaceful feeling the Holy Spirit provided that first time I banged that steering wheel in surrender.

After a year, Pastor Terry resigned. Oh, the heartbreak! He had been such an integral part of my faith journey. A younger preacher was hired–Pastor Cavanaugh—and he would prove to be another kind, God-purposed pastor for my family. He continued to point us to the Lord.

When I didn't know what to do, I asked God. My daily prayers were centered on my boys. I wanted nothing more than their wellbeing and happiness.

"Lead me. Guide me." I begged God. "Help me make sure they get an education."

***

Speaking of the boys and education . . .

With every open house the school scheduled, I made it a priority to attend and begged each of their teachers, "Please let me know if there is anything I can do to help my boy. I want him to have a good education." I often went to the school just to have a five-minute conversation with a teacher. I didn't call ahead or make an appointment. I just went. I wanted to be face-to-face with people. Michael and Robert didn't like it when I showed up after spending all day at the mill. Cotton lint gripped my clothes, and they shook their heads in wonder at how much a mother could embarrass her children. The guidance counselors in middle and high school learned straightaway I had no scruples about ensuring my sons did their best.

"Mom, why do you keep coming to school? We're not in trouble. Only the parents of kids who are in trouble come to the school. We're not giving you any trouble. Why do you have to make friends with all our teachers? Please stop coming!" My boys pleaded with me. We all laugh about it now.

Robert Caviness

So many of my memories of growing up with Mom as a single mother are centered on how she cared for others and us. For example, it seemed she was a famous cook for all the neighborhood kids. Everyone knew Mom would always have freshly cooked rice. Kids showed up in numbers. Often, I would come home from school to a house smelling of Korean food— mostly Kimchi, which is a staple Korean dish consisting of fermented vegetables. Others in the community sent Koreans who had found their way to Randolph County directly to my mom so she could help them get adjusted. Her heart was always steering toward whatever would be of service to others.

Michael Caviness

She was well known at Ramseur Elementary where I went to school from Kindergarten through eighth grade, and it wasn't just for being the only Asian in Ramseur. The teachers knew Suki's boys were going to be well-behaved or she would deal with them. We knew it, too. The teachers learned Mom would always take their sides, and Robert and I would be forced to go back and apologize for our "transgressions." I still see some of my old teachers, and they always ask how my mom is doing.

Mom showed up to all our awards ceremonies at school, having to leave work for an hour to attend each time. She would arrive in her work uniform with lint in her hair, but she was beaming whenever we were recognized. We knew she was proud of us.

Mom always made time for us. Even though she worked twelve-hour shifts, she woke up early to make breakfast for us and often cooked again when she made it home from work in the evenings. She would go out in the yard after dinner or on weekends and play catch with the two of us because she knew we loved baseball. I don't know how she did it. But I'll be forever grateful.

I knew I had to be an example for my boys. I knew they were watching. I registered for an ESL (English as a Second Language) class at the local community college. I hoped to stop embarrassing them with my broken English, and I knew it was one more step toward my goal of being an educated woman.

My friends Charlie and Sue—Sue was also Korean—helped my boys and me tremendously. They were a Christian couple. Charlie knew Michael and Robert needed a positive male influence in their lives, so he stepped in countless times to guide them with their school projects and help with other things we needed around the house. He was like a father to them.

One year, Sue and Charlie invited us to join them on their vacation to Disney World. They had a son three years older than Michael. He was sixteen at the time, so Michael would have been thirteen. It was the week of July 4th. I remember because that was the only full week we had off from the mill.

"Just come with us. We'll take care of the reservations. We have a condo in Daytona Beach for the week. Just come."

Charlie and Sue bought a video camera and paid handsomely for it back then. We loaded up the station wagon, and Sue and Charlie's son drove his little Porsche. The boys rode with him, and loved every minute of the ride down in the fancy sports car. We had never been to Florida before, and that first day, I curled my toes in the sand and giggled with joy. For the next three days we enjoyed all the pleasures of Disney World. Every single parent needs friends like Charlie and Sue. I am so thankful for their love and these memories.

Speaking of people who loved us well, I don't know what I would have done without my friend, Jennifer. Before introducing me to her church, Jennifer was a mother I met at the school's parent group in what they now call the PTO (Parent Teacher Organization). Blonde-headed and down-to-earth, she was a stay-at-home mom with three children. She volunteered at the school often. Her oldest boy was one of Michael's closest friends. Jennifer was one of the few people who didn't look at me and see an Asian. Her eyes and hugs told me she only saw a friend.

After my separation, I spent hours at Jennifer's house talking, crying, and simply sitting with her. It wasn't a fancy house even though the family was financially successful. It was a comfortable, country farmhouse with horses and gardens. Jennifer loved to cook and her house smelled delicious. Jennifer had gone back to school to be an accountant, and every year, we sat in her office and chatted as she did my taxes.

When we weren't figuring out my taxes, we sat in her living room—sometimes her husband was there with us, too. I miss her hugs. She comforted me. We'd chat about anything and everything—kids, marriage, work, and parenting. She listened to my heartbreak and helped me cope with being a single mother in a country I still knew little about. She and her husband were a powerful example of what loving your neighbor means. They never mentioned church—except to introduce me to their church when I was ready—yet their actions showed me God's love.

Michael and Jennifer's son journeyed through high school together. When it was time for us to figure out the college application process, Jennifer was there for me. I didn't know what I was doing. She gave me the deadlines, helped me fill out the applications, and drove us all to tour the various schools. Michael wanted to get away from Ramseur, so he and Jennifer's son both applied to and were accepted at North Carolina State University (NC State) near Raleigh.

I was filled with pride. No one in the Caviness family had ever gone to college. In fact, no one had graduated from high school until the boys' father had earned his diploma in the military back in South Korea. Jennifer's son and Michael were roommates, and like these friends of ours had always done, she and her husband helped us move Michael in when they moved in their own precious boy.

Two years later, Michael's grades were not strong enough to continue at NC State. I believed I had failed him. However, as a mom, I supported his efforts and encouraged him. I was always proud of him.

"Michael, your time at NC State was not a wasted experience."

He came home and promised me he would finish college. He knew he was capable. I knew he could do it, too. He started back at another college closer to our house and lived at home. He also went back to work part-time at the same mill where I worked to earn some spending money.

***

Not long after this, a friend at the mill asked me to go with her to a Gospel concert. When she pulled into my driveway she nonchalantly mentioned we were going to pick up another gentleman who worked at the mill with us who lived down the road from me.

"Okay." I was ambivalent.

The fella's name was John, and I had seen him at the mill, but I didn't realize he lived so close to me—only four houses down. We had never spoken to each other before. He was a tall, older man, easy-going and kind.

John and I learned a lot about each other that night. He was divorced after twenty-five years of marriage and had three grown children. He was raised in the same church we were attending. Most memorably, he was so easy to talk to—spontaneous and witty. I noticed his tender heart too.

After the concert, we waved and said hello at the mill when we passed each other but nothing more. I heard from others he had re-dedicated his life to Christ. I was happy with the news, but honestly, I didn't think much about it at the time.

***

In January 1993, my mother's heart problems led to open-heart surgery. Once she was discharged, I ran back and forth between Asheboro and Ramseur, taking her to appointments.

In March—on top of everything else—Robert and I were involved in a terrible car wreck as we traveled to Asheboro for a friend's house-warming party. Robert was twelve years old. He suffered a chipped tooth and a shoulder injury. His grandparents came to get him because he was released from the hospital that same day. I remained hospitalized for five days with a broken ankle, a crushed heel, and bruised ribs. Michael was a junior in high school and had left for a band competition, so he wasn't in the car. When he heard about the accident, he was afraid we were dead.

Robert Caviness

When I was in the seventh grade, at the start of baseball season, my mom and I were in a head-on collision in front of Randolph Mall. I remember waking up in the car to the sound of my mom screaming and crying out my name. I remember calling for her, though I couldn't move due to torn ligaments in my neck, but I was able to hold her hand and tell her I was okay. She was crying non-stop because the impact of the crash had pushed the motor back onto the heel of her foot and crushed it. It was one of the worst feelings I have ever had—thinking I might lose her and not completely knowing at the time what was happening. Mom was in the hospital for what seemed like two weeks (it was five days) while my brother and I stayed with our grandparents after my discharge from the hospital.

My mother—still on the mend herself—wanted me to stay with her at my brother's house when I was discharged. I worried about her heart. I only stayed for two nights and then decided I was going to my own home. I wanted to take care of Robert, who had been injured as well, and to be with Michael. I wanted to be there for both of them.

The day following my escape to my own home, on a Sunday morning, I woke up to cook our typical Sunday morning breakfast—something hardy. In my stubborn way, I scooted with my walker around the kitchen in excruciating pain. The Lord saw me in my distress and rescued me. My friend, Joyce Kinney, called as I tried to ignore my pain and told me she was coming over with some biscuits. I was so grateful! The members of the church all chipped in and brought our family hot meals every day for the next two weeks. Our Heavenly Father was taking care of us through our friends and church family. In all these ways God loved and sustained us through the generosity of others, and I learned to trust Him and love Him more and more.

My injuries forced me out of work at the mill for four long months. My co-workers told me they would look out for Michael while I was gone. I had found a community of friends at church and at work, and my heart was full despite the lingering sadness

over my broken family and the pain from my broken
ankles.

10 | HARMONY

With each passing Sunday we spent at church, God showed me ways He was redeeming what I had lost. I was able to see all the times He had already worked things out for my good. It felt incredible to live with unveiled eyes. Moving from the Korean Way to the American Way to now, God's Way, I continued to forgive people who had hurt me, and I grew in my faith. God infused peace and harmony into every aspect of my life. But that doesn't mean everything was easy.

While I was home recuperating from the car accident and restricted from doing anything else, my bad habit of smoking—which I had started as a teenager—went into overdrive. I never liked smoking, but I couldn't give it up. It was the last vice from my prior life. People asked me what they should bring me while I was recovering, but I couldn't admit I wanted cigarettes. I just couldn't do it.

But bad habits are tough to break. One day, I called John. He must of thought it was so out-of-the blue since all we had done since the concert was wave to each other at the mill. I suppose it was quite unexpected, but I'm grateful he answered my call.

"Hello? John? It's Suki. Can you bring me cigarettes?"

"I sure can."

He sped to the store, bought a whole carton, and delivered them to me. He didn't want any money for them. I was so grateful, and I wanted to thank him in some way. My physical therapist told me to walk as much as I could. As soon as I was able, I walked to John's house down the street, pushing my walker ahead of me and causing quite a ruckus in our quiet neighborhood.

He lived in a worn, country farmhouse by himself. It had been passed down to him through his parents, and it sat on a sizeable amount of land. When I limped into his driveway, he pulled out some folding chairs from inside the house. We relaxed in the yard and spent more than an hour talking. The neighbors watched us through their windows. We chuckled about that.

After a few visits and when my strength improved, we moved from his yard or porch to the street. We walked around the neighborhood together, still chatting away. The neighbors continued to watch us. Small town gossip is a funny thing. One day John asked me a question I wasn't expecting.

"Do you want to go somewhere? Do you like to travel?"

My kids didn't want me hanging around with them anymore. They were growing up, and they were ready for me to live my own life and for them to live theirs. They were typical teenagers. I knew John fairly well at this point. I knew he was gentle. And I knew he was kind and followed Jesus.

"Sure. Let's go."

I told a couple of my neighbors about our impromptu trip to make sure people knew where I was in case something happened. They laughed and told me John was a good man. I was safe to go with him. So we took off and went fishing. It was the most fun I'd had since my girls' weekend hiking in the South Korean mountains as a teenager.

I had found someone who enjoyed the same things as me—fishing and traveling. John quickly became one of my closest friends. He wanted to do things. See things. But he hadn't had much opportunity to get out and explore when he was younger. Now was his time, and I was thrilled to go with him.

John wanted to spoil me. He liked to talk, but he was just as much a good listener as he was a conversationalist. We laughed a lot. We enjoyed finding new adventures at the beach or in the mountains—anywhere the road and an unfolded map took us. We started dating, but I was hesitant to make any more long-term commitments.

I was hesitant even though I had fallen in love with John. There were many reasons for this—ones I can't explain very well. I guess that's part of love, feeling something indescribable. John promised me he wasn't going to disrupt my relationship with God. He understood the Lord came first. He respected that, and God was first in his life, too. I recalled the time months before when co-workers told me he had rededicated his life to Christ.

John also knew my children came next on my list. Our philosophy was that if our families needed something, we'd stand by them. Supporting both sets of children was important to us. John also told me he understood my relationship with my mother was significant. I was still busy caring for her, taking her to and from medical appointments. He placed himself fourth on the list of my priorities. I never asked him to do that. He intuitively knew at this stage in our lives, we had other commitments that mattered.

But I knew we needed each other in ways neither one of us probably understood until much later. We became the best of friends—companions in life, which God continued to fill with one adventure after another. What else could a woman ask for?

After a few months, John introduced me to his family. His kids were wonderful. We even gathered with his children at Christmas. It would become a tradition in future years.

Robert and Michael liked John. They thought he was "cool." They were witnesses to my happiness and new attitude about life, so they were more than content to leave me to my new relationship. I think it mostly had to do with them finding a measure of relief from my meddling in their lives. Conversely, my older brother did not care for John at first. He believed he was too old for me. His opinion was born out of his desire to protect me.

"You're going to get hurt again."

I didn't think so. Or, maybe I thought it was worth it.

My mom knew John from the mill. Her perspective was different than my brother's.

"If you find someone who is good to you, it doesn't matter what age he is. If you're happy, you go."

***

In 1995, two years into John's and my dating relationship, my mother passed away. Her heart finally gave out. My brother found her unconscious in the yard while some of the family was in the kitchen cooking. We rushed her to the hospital, and she spent the next few fighting for her life. She coded ten times, and the doctors sat us down for a very difficult conversation. We called in other family and the Korean preacher. Despite our aching hearts, we made the impossible decision to stop her life support at 12:00 midnight. I thought my heart might shatter in my chest as I held her hand that evening. Tears dripped onto my clothes and the bed sheets.

"Mom, it's okay to go. We're at peace, Mom."

At 8:00 p.m., my mother passed into Glory. God is so merciful. We didn't have to go through with stopping her care. It was her time, but that didn't make it any easier. It was tough to say goodbye to the matriarch of the family—the one who had worked so hard to keep her children safe through all of life's ups and downs in South Korea. Amidst the grief, the old me tried to resurface, and I fought hard not to view her death as simply part of life. Mother's passing was one of the hardest parts of life.

I still miss her. I was away from her for ten years then she was here for ten years, so I was thankful. I recognized the beauty of it all. I am grateful I had those last ten years for God's redemption, the process of forgiveness, and to tell her how much I loved and appreciated her.

***

My older sister and her family moved to the United States in 1996. It had taken the government ten years to process her whole family for immigration to America. They arrived the year after mother passed and moved to Asheboro. Meanwhile, John and I continued to date, and the neighbors continued to talk.

During the fifth Christmas gathering with John's family in 1997, he proposed to me, giving me a ring in front of his kids. Smiling and pleased, they admitted, "When you didn't get married in the first six months of dating, we didn't think you ever would."

They couldn't believe we were actually going to tie the knot. He and his long-time girlfriend from years ago never married. We had both been single for so long. People thought we were content with our friendship, but we felt so happy together, we wanted to be joined as one.

In May 1998, after five years of dating and just six months after his proposal, John and I married. He wanted to have a beach wedding, but the logistics of getting everyone there became too complicated. I had never had a true wedding, so my family begged for a formal ceremony and celebration. The stress was too much for us to manage with our families and so many different expectations. Off to the courthouse we went with a few fishing buddies and Pastor Cavanaugh, who agreed to marry us despite our histories of divorce. He laughed when we asked him.

"Of course I will! If I don't marry ya'll, someone else will. I should be the one!"

We didn't tell either family about eloping. My boys weren't there. His kids weren't there. After the papers were signed and the witnesses did their jobs, we went out to eat and returned to our respective homes. I called my kids and told them the news. John did the same. When the kids realized we weren't even at the same house after our nuptials, they were confused. They mocked us as if we didn't know what we were doing.

"Go be with your new spouse!" they scolded us through their laughter. We chuckled about it during our honeymoon, which we spent fishing at Ocracoke Island in the Outer Banks of North Carolina—an unincorporated town filled with peaceful days and quiet nights. It was perfect for us.

When we returned from the beach, John moved into my house. Since his house was older and in need of more repairs, he sold it and divided the sale among his family. John also retired that year at age sixty-five after forty-five years at the mill. It was quite an accomplishment.

Our adventures continued. One of his five sisters (he was the youngest of six siblings) had a camper at the beach, and the three of us enjoyed the coastline often. She would stay months at a time since she, too, was retired. I was still working at the mill. On one occasion, when John visited his sister and I was able to go, we took Robert too. John spoiled my kids as much as he spoiled me. It was wonderful.

Robert graduated from high school in June 1998—the month after I married John—and went on to Appalachian State University in western North Carolina. John and I helped him move into his dormitory room, and my heart pumped out a few more beats of pride. Two boys. Two college-educated boys.

A couple months later, after the first semester, Robert came home with some news. He and his girlfriend, Michelle, were pregnant. They were going to have a little girl. At first, I was shocked. I harbored concerns about his college education and how different he and Michelle seemed to be from each other. I was a single mother who raised my boys the best I knew how—in a new culture—and there were times we had barely made ends meet. Michelle had a vastly differently background. She grew up with financial stability. She and her sister had everything they needed.

For a short time after the announcement, I felt pushed out of their lives. Others were catching all the blessings, and I believed the lie that Robert didn't need me anymore. I knew he was shocked and simply trying to do the right thing; I was likely projecting my own failed marriage and the differences between Anthony and me onto Robert's situation. But what could I do? Ultimately, I accepted the news of their pregnancy, and in time, he embraced it too. Robert transferred to The University of North Carolina–Greensboro and found a job at United Parcel Service (UPS). He worked at night, and the company paid his tuition. It was a tremendous blessing.

In March 1999, Adia was born. Oh my! She was precious. Harmony means grandma in Korean. With her birth, I became Harmony. Robert and Michelle decided to get married after her birth, so they had their ceremony at the same time Adia was dedicated to God at three months old. Robert was just nineteen years old. I prayed Robert and Michelle didn't feel trapped by their circumstances and were truly in love.

As our two families were joined together, Michael and Michelle's sister, Dawn, became close— close enough to start dating. In a plan only God could conceive, they were married three years later in

2002. My Korean friends told me I was giving away my two sons to one family. I laughed.

"Well, God will look after us. I want my kids to be happy." I wanted my boys to know I would always be there for them, even though I was in the midst of my own struggles.

11 | GOODBYE

Nearly a year after I married John, we faced unexpected illness. We were camping with his sister, and one morning he started dragging his foot. He was pale. We jumped in the car and when we were halfway home, I kicked him out of the driver's seat. I drove the rest of the way. John refused to go to the doctor. His second eldest son stopped by, and I told him about my concerns.

"Something is wrong, but he's not going to the doctor."

"If he doesn't decide to go by tomorrow morning, call me. I'll make him go."

Angry that another day had gone by, I took John to the doctor the next morning when there was no change. We went to a small clinic, and they transferred John to the hospital. He fought us the whole way. I can only guess he was battling inner fear. Sometimes it's easier not to know. The tests showed he had suffered a light stroke. The doctors kept digging.

One thing led to another, and he underwent a stress test to assess his heart. The results were concerning enough to send him to a larger hospital in Greensboro where he underwent a heart catheterization. By this time, Pastor Cavanaugh and John's other kids had learned of his illness and visited us at the hospital.

Further testing revealed several blockages in his heart. One-third of his heart was already dead.

Apparently, he had suffered a previous heart attack that had gone undetected and untreated, so surgery was no longer an option for John. They prescribed some blood thinners, and I brought him home.

Three weeks later, he awoke to sweating, chest pains, and paleness. I rushed him to the hospital. He had fluid build-up and his kidneys were shutting down. Our fears grew exponentially with each test they performed. The only way he could survive was with home dialysis. Doctors explained he was not a candidate for outpatient dialysis at the hospital because of his deteriorating heart condition.

I was still working twelve-hour shifts at the mill. I took a six-week-long family leave from the mill and participated in a training class to become John's caregiver. A nurse, really.

As with every one of my struggles in life, my old mantra threatened to return: *It is what it is.* I fought that attitude. I was tired of hiding my battles. It broke my heart that John and I had found each other, discovered this happiness, and were enjoying the freedom of traveling and playing in God's nature . . . and then he was sick. It wasn't fair. We had planned so many things to do together—camping trips and other getaways we were forced to cancel. Our carefree weekends became filled with chaos, tubes, and sterile things. I was exhausted. He became diabetic, and I had the added responsibility of giving him the correct amount of insulin. His life was in my hands. But God was with us. He continued to give me peace, despite my tears, nagging fear, and outright frustration.

John stayed on dialysis for six months. Confined to home, his emotional health deteriorated as well. John loved to go, go, go, and this felt like prison to him. No one thought he'd improve. He even sustained another heart attack during those six months. Full healing was not expected, given the severity of his condition.

One morning, John woke up and couldn't move. His muscles were tied up every which way, and it took me an hour to wrap him up and put him in the car to go to the doctor. He was prescribed a steroid and was strangely fine the next day.

My friends, like Jennifer and those in our church community, prayed incessantly. And the good Lord was with us. John kept me laughing through it all. He was such a good patient—and husband! John encouraged me by telling me I was a wonderful caregiver and wife. John used to thank Anthony for making it so easy for him to find happiness. He would tell me my first husband had made a mistake by bringing me over to America and then leaving me even though I was such a magnificent person.

"Someone threw away my treasure." That's what he used to say. My heart skipped a few beats when he whispered those kinds of things to me, as if they were secrets just between us.

But he would never have spoken that way directly to Anthony. John was so gracious to him. We often had family gatherings after Adia was born when we'd all be in the same room together. One such instance, John was going to get coffee and asked Anthony if he'd like one.

During this time while John was ill, Pastor Cavanaugh left our church after ten years, and Pastor Tommy Smith was hired as the new preacher. He re-baptized John on his sick bed and as a special note, was the one who married Michael and Dawn in 2002.

With John's compliments and our friends' prayers, I watched miracles happen. After six months, his kidneys responded and their function improved enough for him to come off dialysis. His doctors were amazed, and of course we attributed it all to our Heavenly Healer.

Once the dialysis ended, John was ready to go again. I was more than willing to go with him. With every short break I had from the mill, he waited at home for me to finish my shift, and when I walked through the door, I knew to be ready to go somewhere.

He bought a JEEP and we packed our picnic basket and cooler. John and I traveled all over the Eastern seaboard—mostly fishing up and down the coast. There were many days we spent lingering at the beach. It was glorious—such a gift.

John had six sisters—he was the youngest of them all—and we visited with them, too, on these excursions. They were so generous. His family was a true community. His sisters had prayed for him when he was sick. I knew the Spirit of God was with all of us, and I knew God had answered our prayers. It was the reason we had this extra time together. I'm so thankful we fully enjoyed his short recovery; it ended too soon.

John passed away in April 2003. His heart failed him. He had gained a lot of weight with all the medications and the diabetes diagnosis. He had been in and out of the hospital for the last forty months of his life. His family was so appreciative of how I stood by him. They told me because I cared for him and loved him as well as I did, he had lived those extra three years. That meant the world to me.

It seemed all those whom I loved struggled with heart problems that ended up destroying them in the end. First was my aunt in the Korean countryside, then my mother, and now my husband. I knew God would give me extra strength for this season of my life. I felt God was in the heartache, stitching pieces together every time they tore apart. And this tear was a big one.

John had never been able to tolerate it when people were mistreated. His ability to connect with those in need was unparalleled. He saw people as God did—as children of the Almighty. John never had to introduce himself to anyone in our town. Everyone knew him. He was part of the fabric of our small community, a beloved staple. When I was with him, I belonged. I was connected. When we married, my community tripled. People knew to whom I belonged—God . . . and John. At his funeral, 300 more people showed up than we expected. It was wall-to-wall full of tearful faces. It took me five hours to greet everyone; I wasn't going to miss or ignore a single soul. This was a testimony to the type of person John was.

Once John was gone, I kept busy remodeling our house, and I continued to work at the mill until 2008. I took a forced retirement after twenty-eight years when the mill closed down, and I said goodbye to all the friends I had made there. I entered the next season of my life, one filled with my boys and their growing families.

12 | MANY HOMES

In 2005, I finished remodeling my little house and had just cleaned everything up when another tidal wave of heartbreak hit. I wish Robert and Michelle's marriage had been filled with harmony when I became Harmony. Instead, I watched it unravel.

"Robert, you are growing in a different direction than Michelle."

He didn't disagree. Unfortunately, it wasn't meant to be, and one day, Robert left Michelle. His choice to do so catapulted me back to the weekend Anthony had walked out on our family. I was devastated. I knew the emotional toll of divorce all too well. This time my boy was the one abandoning his family.

I begged Robert to reconsider, but he had made up his mind. It just destroyed me—having that first-hand knowledge of how they all must be hurting. It was more painful this time than when I was the abandoned spouse staring at the empty half of the bed. I cried for a week. I cried mostly for my grandchildren. Adia was six and Aiden, her new brother, was just three months old.

In my anger and despair, I ran Robert off. I told him to go find somewhere else to stay. He lived in a fire station for a short time, but then he turned to his father. He had previously changed careers from teaching to fire fighting. He lived at his dad's until my raw emotions cooled and I changed my mind.

"If you bring those kids to my house on the days you have them, I'll help you. But you're taking care of them. I just want to make sure they aren't mistreated anywhere else."

I was thinking of random friends or sitters Robert would have relied on if I were not willing to help. I couldn't tolerate the thought of the kids being bounced around from one place to another. Robert moved in with me so he could have a safe and stable place to bring Adia and Aiden while he and Michelle shared custody. However, I set some ground rules:

"No drinking. No monkey business. You be a good father."

Robert Caviness

I found myself leaning on Mom as a twenty-five-year-old kid going through a divorce with two kids of my own. Mom begged me to work it out with my now ex-wife, not realizing the struggles I had faced. She even kicked me out of the house in desperate hope of forcing me to further work on my marriage. She did eventually let me live with her but not until I went through a stint of sleeping at fire stations and on my dad's couch.

She became supportive, inviting me to go fishing with her at the beach during my separation, just so I could get away and clear my head from all the rumors running rampant about me in a small town. Mom's words lifted me at that time and still ring true today: "Continue to be a good dad and do what is right in the eyes of the Lord, and people will see you for who you really are." She was affirming me for who I was—a good person—and it meant the world to me.

Living with Suki as an adult was not easy, especially when I had my two kids with me, which was half the time. To begin with, Mom wanted me to follow rules as if I was a teenager again. Somehow we managed to make things work. Thankfully, she was there no matter what, to give me advice and help me become a better parent. I know now that Mom was just trying to save me from some of the heartache she had endured as the result of her own separation and divorce. It took me twenty-five years to realize my mother was one of the smartest women I have ever known. I am forever grateful.

Dawn and Michael moved in with Michelle to help her after the separation. At this point, I felt the kids were going to have enough family support to be okay. We all made our choices with the kids' hearts, minds, and futures at stake.

Adia Caviness

It's a funny thing that I cannot remember much from my parents' divorce, but what I do remember is I had a home at Harmony's. She converted my Uncle Michael's old bedroom into Aiden's and my new second home. I decorated my half in pink with horse memorabilia, while Aiden's side was littered with trucks. Harmony became a second mother to us. While I lived with my mom, aunt, and uncle half the time in the big house, I spent the other half of my days in Harmony's Korean house. It was cool to have two houses to call my own, both safe and filled with love, but starkly different in other ways. At my mom's house, we ate out nearly every night. At Harmony's, she cooked every night. I ate my fair share of home-cooked meals as well as special, fancy food from the local Chinese restaurant.

Harmony bathed me until I was almost ten years old. It was one of my favorite things in the world. Harmony would draw a warm bath, and I sat in that green tub and relaxed alone for a while. Then, she would enter the bathroom and wash my hair. It was a delightful process. First came the washing and then the conditioning. Nothing feels better than a Korean woman running her fingers through your hair to scrub every strand clean. Just thinking about it gives me chills. We joke about the bath times to this day and ask one another if it would be weird for her to give me a bath now that I'm nineteen. It would be, but I would secretly love it. Harmony still braids my hair and gives me spa treatments—facemasks. These moments in time have become some of my favorites.

Looking back now, I realize how hard it must have been for Harmony to open her home to two young children and my father. Yet, she did it with grace and love. Though Harmony and I disagreed over things throughout the years, she was always on my side. I knew I could count on her, and that security blessed me in ways she may not ever realize.

Robert and I kept our arrangement for seven years. During that time, I fulfilled another lifelong dream—securing an education. I completed my high school equivalents and earned my GED. It wasn't easy, but it was worth finishing.

Adia Caviness

Harmony wanted me to be a good student—eager to learn. She bought me workbooks for extra practice. To make her proud, I completed all of them. Harmony worked towards her GED when I was in the third and fourth grades.

One day, she and I sat at the kitchen table, doing our homework side-by-side. She turned to me and asked me how to do a math problem, and I acted like I knew. She made me feel like a teacher. I am certain I didn't understand the problem she was doing, but it meant so much to me that she was willing to ask for my advice. She valued my opinion, even though I was young. I felt special and smart, and this memory has stuck with me all these years. Now, when I help students as a Teacher's Assistant at North Carolina State University, I experience those same feelings. When students ask for my help, I feel emboldened, empowered, and loved. It all began with Harmony's faith in my knowledge, my ability to teach, and in me.

When Adia turned thirteen, my house became too cramped for us all. After a series of decisions—ones dictated only by our obedience to God—I sold my house to Robert and moved to a new one in Franklinville, North Carolina. I was delighted to keep my pretty, little house in the family. There were countless big memories attached to such a small structure. God led me through the new house hunting process, too. Though, it took longer than I thought it would.

Originally, I purchased a new house that needed fixing up. I spent two years relentlessly doing more renovations. One day during Sunday school, my friend Yvonne told me the house next door to hers was for sale. Her neighborhood was beautiful. I loved everything about, including the fact that Charles Kinney and his wife also lived there. I loved everything about it except the cost. I assumed it was outside my price range.

"I can't afford that house!"

"Just come look at it."

I went. I looked. I fell in love, as I knew I would. It needed a little work, but I felt God was telling me to do something with it. Joyce's husband, Charles, had passed away. It was my turn to be the friend and neighbor she had been to me for so long. It was my turn to offer her a place and a shoulder to find fellowship amidst her grief and loneliness.

My brothers thought I was crazy to even consider owning two houses. But, the financing was easy. Shortly after touring the house, God made the way for the price to drop, and I decided to go for it. Through His mighty Providence, someone quickly offered to buy my house. So on one spectacular day, I sold a house and thirty minutes later, I bought one. God was so good to me. I was just along for the ride.

I looked back through my childhood and young adult years dreaming about, saving up for, and hunting for homes. The ups and downs, the twists and turns—only a Heavenly Father looking out for his beloved child could have arranged everything the way it all happened. After all, I didn't even know how to fill out a college application, let alone buy and sell so many houses. I knew in the depths of my soul He had planned my life around not just the hunt for houses, but the concept of *home*.

In 2018, after working short stints at a hospital and another mill, I completely retired. My brother was thrilled to hear I finally stopped working.

"You need to get out. Take a break. Rest. You've done good, Sister."

Today, I am content on the path He has for me in my "golden years." It's a new purpose in this new season of life. I help my boys and their families with taking care of my grandchildren and cleaning. I enjoy watching my boys—who are wonderful men, both firefighters, fathers, and children of God—growing into their own purposes. I take pride in how many people love and respect them. Michael and Dawn have two children: Cole and Cadence. Both exude joy with a pinch of sass. I like to think I may have had a little something to do with the sass part. God gives them their joy. As I write this memoir, Adia is in Africa on mission and Aiden is growing up fast, too. I love being a witness to their self-discovery and growing relationships with God.

All my grandchildren know the love of both earthly fathers and their Heavenly Father. Now, I've come full circle. I started my life dreaming of a home. I spent the majority of my years striving for a home. I married, crossed an ocean, toiled at a mill, married again, and lost many loved ones during my search for home. I've bought and sold four homes and renovated three of them during that journey. I stumbled and fell along the way, but I ultimately discovered the Way, the Truth, and the Life—the One who bridges the gap between where I am now and my eternal home. My life-long hunt for home is over. I found the King of Kings. The Good News is the peace of knowing my real home is not here on earth but in Heaven and the assurance of to Whom I belong will satisfy me forever.

SUKI'S PRAYER

There are many more stories and people to thank. I could write forever. I chose to end this memoir with Scripture and a prayer that sums up the gratitude I have for others in my life.

Psalm 121
A song of ascents.

I lift up my eyes to the mountains—
where does my help come from?
My help comes from the Lord,
the Maker of heaven and earth.
He will not let your foot slip—
he who watches over you will not slumber;
indeed, he who watches over Israel
will neither slumber nor sleep.
The Lord watches over you—
the Lord is your shade at your right hand;
the sun will not harm you by day,
nor the moon by night.
The Lord will keep you from all harm—
he will watch over your life;
the Lord will watch over your coming and going
both now and forevermore.

Heavenly Father,

You are my rock and my fortress. Even when I didn't know You—didn't know to lift my eyes up to

You—You helped me. Your hand was over me, guiding me onto the path that would lead me to You. There are so many people You commissioned along the way, positioning them in my life and pointing me to You. I pray for each and every person who was an instrument of Your goodness and mercy.

Lord, I lift up the entire community of Ramseur, North Carolina in thanksgiving. From the Ramseur Wesleyan Church to Ramseur Elementary School and everyone in-between, they opened their arms to me—a Korean-American—and my family and supported us at every turn. God, I pray some day they can understand how the magnitude of grace and encouragement they offered us made such a difference in our lives.

Father, I thank You from the bottom of my heart for Ramtex Mill. You made a way for me to find lasting friendships and meet the love of my later life, John. Only You, in all Your creativity and resourcefulness, could use a mill to make beauty from ashes.

God, I offer a prayer of gratitude to my Korean family. To my mother in Heaven, my father whom I adored, and my siblings who made me feel less alone, I pray a heartfelt thank You. Lord, guide my brothers, sisters, and me as we continue to navigate this world and make our way Home. To You be the glory.

Heavenly Father, how can I ever thank You for my boys, Michael and Robert. I cry when I think about how they have blessed me. I may be their mother, but they have taught me so much. From the bottom of my heart, I ask You keep Your guiding hand over them forever and ever.

The Scotton Family has been a Godsend family. They have gifted me with two women, the mothers of my four grandchildren—Adia, Aiden, Cole, and Cadence. God, thank you for Cheryl—Michelle and Dawn's mother—a good friend. And why not? We're all family. Lord keep the Scottons close and satisfied with Your everlasting love.

Dawn, my daughter-in-law and Michael's beloved wife . . . Lord you created this woman and made her perfectly adventurous, tenderhearted, and an exceptional listener. She's willing to jump in and try anything, including some of my favorite Korean recipes. As I shared some of these stories with her before I put pen to paper and wrote this memoir, she simply sat and cried. She, more than anyone, can feel others' pain though it's not directly her own. This can only be because of Your Spirit in her. Her compassion for others is not unlike the compassion John had before he went Home.

Father, I miss my friend Jennifer. I'm not sure she realized how much she impacted me. Thank you for bringing her into my life. She was just the right person at just the right time. I know you two must be dancing together right now.

Lord, please hold Joyce Kinney tight for me until I can see her again. She accepted me, included me, and encouraged me as You taught her to do. She was such a good and faithful servant, and she changed my life.

Along with Joyce, God I pray blessings over Sue and Charlie. The way you weaved people like these through my life is a testament to Your unending love for us all. They deserve a special place in Heaven for pointing me to Jesus through their words and actions. I have been blessed beyond measure.

Looking back at my life, I can see so many ways I missed You but You never lost sight of me. As one of my favorite hymns, "Through It All" by Andraé Crouch, summarizes, we have difficult times, we shed some tears, and we may have questions, but despite all of that, we can trust You and rest in Your promises. I pray those reading my memoir go and listen to this hymn and their eyes are opened to Your steadfast nature and truly understand they can depend on Your faithfulness.

God, You are majesty and love and grace. You gift us with blessings and turn our difficult stories into beautiful memoirs. As long as we lean into You, we cannot be undone. We cannot be lost. We will find Home.

In Jesus's precious name,
Suki

FAMILY PHOTOS

Large Mansion that was converted after the Korean War to be used partially for a basic school, while other rooms of building were rented out as homes for individual families. Maternal Aunt and Cousins rode on boat with Choon Pil Moon to escape North Korea and during war were in same refugee camp.

Left to right: Choon Pil Moon (Mother), Kuk Hyung Han (Baby), Chung Yeol Han (Father), Chun Nun Moon (Maternal Aunt), Kyong Suk Han Richardson, Kyung Ja Han (Sister), Tuk Som Saw (Maternal Cousin), Kyung Ok Han (Baby), Kyung Sum Saw (Cousin)

1970 - 15 Years Old, 1st restaurant
job, taking an order

1971 School Photo - 17 Years Old

1971 School Photo - 17 Years Old

1975 - Anthony Caviness, 1st year of
marriage, back in the U.S.

1975 - Korea - Washing dishes at the
water pump

1978 - In Korea just before coming back to the
U.S. Michael, 1.5 years old in Daddy's army
boots

1980 - Newport News, VA - Robert, age 2
months, Michael, age 3.5

1980 - Military Wife

1983- Visiting mother in
Korea at Korean Folk Town

1984- Robert 4 years
old), Michael (8 years old)

1987- Kuk Hyung Han (25 years old), Il Hyung Han (21 years old)

1st year at family Korean United Methodist Church in Greensboro, at Christmas, singing in church.
Left to right: Il Hyung Han (Brother), Kuk Hyung Han (Brother), Suki, Robert, Michael, Choon Pil Moon

1998 - 2nd marriage to John Lewis Richardson at Ramseur Wesleyan Church

Present day - Grandchildren Adia, Cole, Cadence, and Aiden

ABOUT THE AUTHOR

Kyong Suk Han Richardson (Suki) is the proud daughter of two North Korean refugees. She grew up in post-war South Korea. In 1975, as a young military wife, she moved to the United States to a small rural southern town in central North Carolina. It was in this small town of Ramseur that she raised her two sons, learned to speak English with a southern accent, and became one of the hardest workers at the local textile mill. Although she has worked in the textile industry most of her life, she now spends each day caring for her grandchildren. She enjoys cooking— both traditional southern food and Korean food— tending to her backyard garden, and spending time with her family, friends and her church community. *The Hunt for Home* is her personal memoir where she outlines her adventurous life and shares the way God has been with her and her family through her entire life's journey.

CPSIA information can be obtained
at www.ICGtesting.com
Printed in the USA
LVHW031048301120
672995LV00003B/159